DebtOcracy
& Odious Debt Explained

MAINE PATRIOT. COM
3 Linnell Circle
Brunswick, Maine 04011

maine-patriot.com

DebtOcracy
& Odious Debt Explained
CONTENTS

DebtOcracy

Definition

odious. adj. exciting or deserving hatred or repugnance. syn. HATEFUL.

odious debt. n. unconscionable debt deserving hatred or repugnance.

DebtOcracy

Easy Solution to Greek Woes: Repudiate Its Unpayable Debt

By Peter Papaherakles, AMERICAN FREE PRESS, July 11, 2011, ISSUE 28, WWW.AMERICANFREEPRESS.NET

As Greece is being led into financial enslavement by a corrupt government in bed with the global banking cartels, increasing numbers of economists are saying that rather than sinking deeper into debt it can never repay, Greece should take control of its destiny and repudiate the unconstitutional debt that it has been saddled with.

Although writers in the alternative press have been floating this suggestion for months, mainstream economists are also starting to say the same thing lately.

On June 16, even Allen Mattich of the *Wall Street Journal* wrote an article entitled "Greece May View Euro Exit; Debt Default as Best Option in Financial Crisis."

Mattich stated, "Greeks are fed up with austerity and seem unwilling to take on the still stricter conditions being demanded of them. Were the Greeks to decide that a euro-exit is not only possible, but desirable, the core EU, led by Germany, would almost certainly make huge concessions, including debt forgiveness. A Greek default and departure from the euro would risk a systemic crisis across Europe's financial sector."

Economic analyst Max Keiser calls the bankers criminals and suggests that Greece bring back the drachma. He sees what is going on in Greece as part of a worldwide problem of unscrupulous bankers conquering the world through debt.

DebtOcracy, a new documentary film by Constas Lapavitsas, an economist and professor in London, makes the best case for repudiating the debt. According to reports, over a million Greeks have seen it on the Internet. A very well-made film, it introduces the concept of "odious debt" established in the 1920's by Russian economist Alexander Sack.

Several countries have used this concept to repudiate unconstitutional debts throughout history, including Ecuador, which only paid 20 cents on the dollar to cover its debt a few years ago.

When the United States occupied Iraq in 2003, they inherited a $120 billion debt that Iraq owed to Russia and France. They declared the debt odious, and the United States did not repay a dime.

An odious debt conforms to three qualifications: 1. The government receives the loan without the people's approval; 2. The loan is spent for activities not beneficial to the people; and 3. The lender is aware of the above yet lends the money anyway, thus committing a hostile act against the people of the target country.

In Greece's case, the whole financial crisis was created by fraud between Wall Street, the IMF, European bankers, and corrupt Greek politicians over the past decade. The Greek people clearly do not benefit from these loans as they merely pay for interest on previous loans.

As a matter of fact, no real money was ever loaned anyway. Rather, ledger entries were made marking interest payments as paid. Not a penny of the $150 billion has actually gone to help the people of Greece. Finally, the lenders were complicit in defrauding the people of Greece.

The entire financial crisis was manufactured and sold to the public through hype created by the banker-owned international media, with politicians playing scripted roles. The whole thing is a Hollywood production, with the people of Greece serving as hapless victims.

If the United States Government doesn't dramatically curb ITS spending, we Americans will be victims in a future episode just like this one.

The banker-owned media places the blame on a bloated bureaucracy and crippled tax system. The clever PIIGS acronym (Portugal, Ireland, Italy, Greece, Spain) was crafted to convey the misconception that Greece and other countries are lazy gluttons that squandered mountains of cash.

DebtOcracy documents show that bankers and politicians engaged in wasteful projects in which they benefited while bringing Greece into bankruptcy. These included bribes and kickbacks from German conglomerate Siemens to build the Athens subway system, in addition to huge spending for the 2004 Olympics.

Even worse was many billions for high-priced weapons like airplanes and submarines bought from European manufacturers owned by the same bankers. This type of fiscal manipulation is textbook *Economic Hitman* material as described by author John Perkins in his book by that name.

Greece is the canary in the mine in a bankers' End Game. If Greece goes down, it won't be long before the United States goes down.

DebtOcracy

INTRODUCTION
DebtOcracy (2011)

The following is a Transcript of a 2011 documentary film by Katerina Kitidi and Aris Hatzistefanou, that mainly focuses on two points:

1. the causes of the Greek debt crisis in 2010 and
2. possible solutions to the problem that are not currently being considered by the government of Greece.

The documentary opens with the statements of Greek Prime Ministers, starting with dictator Georgios Papadopoulos, and the then managing director of the International Monetary Fund, Dominique Strauss-Kahn; and ends with comments from some of the most prominent figures in Greek politics since the Metapolitefsi: Andreas Papandreou; Konstantinos Mitsotakis; Kostas Simitis; Kostas Karamanlis; and current Prime Minister George Papandreou.

The focus then shifts to the prelude to the recent global economic crisis and its origins in the 1970s.

Interviews with prominent figures of the global philosophical and economic scene also point to the non-viability of the euro and its contribution to the worsening of the finances of Greece due to a systematic loss of competitiveness in the markets by the so-called PIIGS. [Portugal, Italy, Ireland, Greece, and Spain].

The documentary claims that the euro has contributed to the crisis.

The documentary traces the roots of the Greek debt back to the revolution of 1821 and the British loans that were issued at that time. The documentary points out that Greece, in its 190 years of existence, has only lent money once, during the German occupation of Greece, and has always been the borrower of loans in all other instances.

The documentary asserts that the current debt of Greece is due to the nationalization of failing private companies, the systematic failure of the state to tax fairly, the restrictions of the Maastricht treaty, the new loans that were issued to pay off older debts, and the current economic policies of Greece, the IMF, and the ECB, which will result in an even higher debt, equal to 167% of the country's GDP in 2013, if not discharged.

Discover the real causes of the Economic Crisis striking every country in the world today, how and why it happened, and where it's headed today.

This documentary is presented in the Greek language with subtitles in English.

A Link to view the documentary is provided at the end.

1
Justification For Theft

Georg Papadopoulos, Dictator: *"Yet once shall I attempt a comparison with doctors. We have a patient; we've placed him in a plaster cast."*

Dominique Strauss-Kahn, IMF Managing Director: *"Don't decide against the doctor, sometimes the doctor gives you a medicine you don't like, but even if you don't like the medicine, the doctor is there to try to help you."*

As has been said before, history has this wicked habit of repeating itself as a force. So, from a dictator/wannabe-doctor, we move on to the MD's of the IMF.

Andreas Papandreou, Prime Minister of Greece, 1981-1990, 1993-1996: *"Everybody has to join in the struggle, fully aware that either the nation will obliterate its huge debt, or the huge debt will obliterate the nation."*

Constantinos Misotakis, Prime Minister of Greece, 1990-1993: *"This year's income policy will be strict and austere. No raises will be given whatsoever."*

Costas Simitis, Prime Minister of Greece, 1996-2004. *"There is no more room for benefits or tax cuts."*

Costas Karamanlis, Prime Minister of Greece, 2004-2009: *"We have to cut public spending, we have to tidy up our house. And this cannot be achieved with your empty promises of handing out money and privileges at a time of such crisis."*

Giorgos Papidreou: Prime Minister of Greece. *"Unfortunately, our country is in the ICU. The nation's fiscal deadlock threatens our sovereignty for the first time since 1974.*

In the past 40 years, two political parties, 3 families of politicians along with certain businessmen, led the country to bankruptcy. They declared suspension of payments to the people, in order to save their lenders.

After decades of continuous austerity, the Czars of the economy advertised Greece as the local financial superpower.

Yannos Papantronious, Minister of France, 1994-200: *"Our work is great. We were the first to solve the economic problems."*

N. Christodoulakis, Minister of Finance, 2001-2004: *"Once more, our economy will prove to be our strongest asset."*

Yannos Papantonious, Minister of Finance, 1994-2001: *"The economy sprang forward and went from second to first league.*

When their creation crumbled, those people said behind our back that, due to some genetic disorder, we were incapable of handling our economy without foreign aid. Perhaps Americans may find it difficult to understand this. But Greece lacks ability in the control of debt and discipline.

Our government called us bums, and our lenders, PIIGS,

as was the case with all peripheral EU countries. And our ministers tried to convince us that all of us had a part in this.

Brian Lenihan, Ireland's Minister of Finance, 2008-2011: *"I accept that we failed in our political system, but let's be fair about it, we're all part of it."*

Theodores Pangalos, Vice President of the Greek Government: *"The answer to the denouncement of the country's politicians that make people ask us, What did you do with the money? is: We made you civil servants! We all had a part in this!"*

So we are the prodigal children of a neat global economy in an all-successful Europe? Or has the system been ailing since its youth?

Clip: The Chamber of Commerce of the United States presents, "It's Everybody's Business": "Capitalist economy in the post-war period consists of two parts."

Costas Lapavitsas, Professor of Economics: *"In the first 25 years after World War II, the growth rate was high. Real income rose, as did the consumption of goods. Those were novel circumstances in the history of capitalism. Joe is king, because he can buy more with his wages than any other worker on the blow."*

David Harvey, Social Scientist: *"There's no such thing as a crises free capitalism. So, there's gonna be a crisis somewhere."*

This happy period ended in the mid-Seventies. From then on, we entered a period of low growth, recurrent crises, suppressed if any rises in workers' income, — and high unemployment. Mature capitalists countries found it difficult to accrue wealth.

David Harvey, Social Scientist: *"The crisis was really focused on the power of Labor which was very strong at that time in the core capitalist regions in Europe and North America, and the result of that, there was a lot of pressure on wages. Labor was organized. They had a lot of power and state elections, so they had to discipline Labor. And they didn't, in a number of ways. They did it mainly by opening up national economies to global competition, gaining access to the world's favor, resources, and eventually of course, China came into the picture [willing to work for much less compensation]."*

Financialisation brought on and intensified the crisis.

Capital could go very much to where it wanted to take advantage of low Labor. But then the problem arose that the share of wages and national income was going down everywhere. And or course wages is a big part of the market.

So then it became a problem of how can you sell your goods when the purchasing power is not there. And the answer was, "give" [loan] everybody credit. So we got the invention of the "credit" [debt] economy which really picks up strongly in the 1980's and 1990's to **cover the gap between what Labor was actually getting in wages and what it could actually purchase.*** And that's when many people began to see by the end of the 1990's-2000 that this was the unsustainable bit. The way we got out of the crisis of the 1970's prepared the ground for this kind of crisis.

When the US housing bubble burst the world financial system came close to total collapse. As a result it affected the real economy, which has its own structural problems.

State took rescue measures. They used tax-payers' money. Thus, the financial crisis went fiscal. And those same banks which were saved by the tax-payers decided to bite the hand that fed them, by gambling on state bankruptcies.

Speculation made things worse in Greece, too. Only this time, the problem is even deeper. It's time for the Eurozone to pay. King Euro proves naked, mainly because he's a king without a state.

*The solution to **"covering the gap between what Labor was actually getting in wages and what it could actually purchase"** can be seen by considering *the Principles of Personal Credit* explained in the author's books *"From Debt to Prosperity; 'Social Credit' Defined"* and *"Give Yourself Credit: Money Doesn't Grow On Trees."*
See Chapters 8 and 14 of this book.

DebtOcracy

2
Economic Explanations

Samir Amin: Economist: *"There cannot be a currency without a state. Despite their weaknesses, the advantage of the US dollar, among other things, is that there is a state called the USA. Europe does not exists as a political entity. There's no legitimatized political power connecting its states. In my opinion the Eurozone is not viable."*

In contrast to the USA, where the federal government and the Federal Reserve System intervene to ameliorate inequalities among states, the Eurozone accentuates inequality. This is how the PIIGS, the poor relatives of the EU, Portugal, Italy, Ireland, Greece and Spain, came into existence.

The Eurozone is divided distinctly into Central and peripheral states. The crisis is more intense in the peripheral states. The central states, especially Germany, are winners because of the euro.

The competitiveness of EU states came to vary a lot, and the competition of peripheral countries fell steadily and systematically behind. This was directly due to the euro.

Eric Toussaint, President of the Commission for the Abolition of Third World Debt: *"The crisis in the EU was a result of the way Europe was integrated."*

With Greece, it's like putting Muhammed Ali, the World Heavyweight Champion, in the Ring with a featherweight boxer, and telling them: Start fighting and let's see who wins.

Why are the peripheral countries lagging behind in competitiveness? Most of all, what causes this divergence to keep increasing?

The myth of the "lazy" peripheral, and "industrial" Germany with its "high productivity", is just that. All the German government managed was to declare war on their own workforce and freeze their salaries for a decade.

Sahra Wagenknecht, Deputy Chairperson, Die Linke: *"In recent years, the nominal increase in salaries was 7% in Germany while in the Eurozone it was 27%. This gap logically results in loss of competitiveness in other countries, when salaries go down in one country, while they go up in all the others, while the other countries are unable to follow. The Eurozone countries are no longer able to devaluate their currency. This resulted in the establishment of a mechanism which was bound to lead to the results we have today."*

Costas Lapavitsas, Professor of Economics: *"The loss of competitiveness manifested itself in two ways, both of which played a decisive part in the crisis. Firstly, great defects occurred in current transactions. And Greece had the greatest deficit of all. When you're unable to compete, your transactions with the rest of the world result in a deficit. And Greece's deficit is huge. But this goes for the other peripheral countries as well. This phenomenon went hand-in-hand with the accruing of debt. If you have such deficits, you must balance them somehow."*

Samir Amin: Economist: *"In the EU, Greece is the poor relative. Greece belongs to the European continent's semi-peripheral countries. It's evident that Greece was bound to accrue national debt given circumstances of its integration into European markets. I won't even bother with the rumor that Greeks are lazy. That's pure racism."*

The Eurozone destroys the immune system of peripheral countries leaving them exposed to the global crisis. The Achilles' heal of those countries is deficit and debt. In our case, the debt is rooted deep in the history of the Greek state.

Manolis Glezos, historical figure of the Greek left: *"From the time of The Revolution of 1821, our country started borrowing, and its been borrowing ever since. With one exception. During an extraordinary "Happy" period, Greece managed to become a lender. During the German Occupation, Greece lent to Germany. The Germans forced Greece to become a lender, instead of a borrower. After the German Occupation ended, the country resumed its traditional role; that of a borrower. And national debt as we know it, started to rise in the 1980's."*

Costas Lapavitsas, Professor of Economics: *"The high levels of national borrowing in Greece relate to Greece's social and class structure and the form that the Greek economy has assumed over the last few decades. It has to do with the Greek state's systematic inability to implement an effective and fair system of taxation."*

Clip: "History of Greek Sovereignty Defined": *"Andreas Papandreou created the necessary welfare state without increasing corporate and high income taxes. He saved jobs by nationalizing loss-making private companies. Primarily, though, he saved the companies' owners. Public deficit and sovereign debt increased dramatically. Mitsitakis' government continued to borrow. The Maastricht treaty imposed world markets as the only mechanizm for deficit control, prohibiting other means of money creation. Debt skyrocketed with the highest increase rate in Greek history. Kostas Simitis was luckier [creative accounting]. The fall of European interest rates and economic growth were on his side, that he placed on sovereign debt. During his premiership, the percentage of debt seemed to decrease slightly, Kostas Karamanlis decreased capital taxation by 10%. The economic free fall accelerated, and debt exploded once more."*

End of Clip.

3
Argentina & The Debt Trap

Most countries in a similar situation were visited by the IMF. But none paid as dearly as Argentina; Greece's mirror image on the other side of the Atlantic.

Argentina fell into the debt trap at the same time as did Greece, in 1824, with the first British loans. But the noose tightened towards the end of the 20th century. Argentina locked the rate of its peso against the US dollar. This made it impossible for them to exercise a monetary policy. Argentina experienced its own Eurozone. Only instead of Berlin they were up against Washington DC.

M. Candessus, IMF Managing Director, 1987-2000: ***"It's a way to enter the new century on a very solid basis."***

At the same time, the IMF turned the country into yet another experimental laboratory for Neo-liberalism .

Excerpt from the documentary film, "The Take", Avi Lewis, Film-maker, Journalist: ***"First of all the IMF played a signature role creating the crisis in Argentina, during the policies of deregulation and privatizing that led to immense corporate profits, that really destroy the finances of a state."***

After Argentina's economic collapse in 2001, Argentina became the laughing stock of economists all over the world. But some monsters never die. The IMF is something like a zombie institution. You can't kill it. The IMF has reemerged as a player in, quote, quietly bailing out countries that get into trouble, imposing austerity conditions, as is happening across Europe, in a vicious and terrifying way indeed, and there is no sense whatsoever that this institution has learned anything from the experience of Argentina.

Greece will pay dearly for the intervention of the IMF. And in some cases, she will even pay for it in advance.

Ron Paul, Republican Congressman: *"The irony of this promise is that in the new arrangement of this increase, Greece is going to put 2.5 billion dollars in there. I think that's only a fiat monetary system worldwide to come up and have Greece help bail out Greece and be prepared to bail out even other countries."*

Argentina was confronted by the IMF, alone. But Greece found herself serving two masters. Because in Europe, Neoliberal theories were also being promoted by the European Central Bank. The European Central Bank was a tool, you know.

Ironically enough, in the case of Greece, the IMF was softer than the EU. The measures applied in collaboration with the IMF, the ECB and the EU are not only unfair and dangerous to the Greek people, they were also deemed to fail right from the start. They have a tragic impact on the peoples' quality of life, and on their daily life even. And it's highly unlikely that they will have a positive effect on the economy in general and the management of the national debt.

Like in Argentina, the target was to save not the economy, but rather the banks and the big enterprises.

The IMF put magnificent pressure on Argentina to repay these debts. Many of the debts were inflated, in fact exploded, because of the transfer of debt from huge corporations, including some of the biggest banks in the world, onto the public treasury, onto the public purse, which the IMF pushed for as well.

The measures taken now, are stabilization measures to prevent Greece from proceeding to a cessation of due payments. They are not measures which will reduce the debt. It is more than obvious that the debt will continue to increase gradually, regardless of the measures, and indeed as a result of them. The measures are clearly to protect the lenders and to protect the banks.

Within a few months, the Greek government gave the banks 108 billion euros which is almost the entire rescue package received from the IMF and the EU.

Excerpt from the documentary film, Social Genocide: *When Argentina faced a similar situation several of those responsible were punished. The image of presidents' leaving the presidential palace in choppers still haunts both the IMF and its collaborators.*

One magical night, just like in Argentina, we'll see who gets to hop into the chopper first. Greece has entered an intensive program of "purging" procedures, "asset utilization", "rationalization" and "tidying up." The delegates of the IMF, the EU, and the ECB have taken upper-management residence in Athens, and are dictating their policy through an unconstitutional memorandum.

Dominique Strauss-Kahn, IMF Managing Director: *"The main question now is to align wages and productivity."*

What is Greece today? Are we a free country? Yes. Are we independent? No. We've been reduced to vassals. Freedom is one thing. Sovereignty in quite another thing. Our country's problem is that she has lost her sovereignty.

N. Kanakis, President, Doctors of the World, Greece: *"In splendid collaboration with their foreign lenders, the government has turned against the people with harsh measures. We consider the centre of Athens to be facing a humanitarian crisis. All the distictive features are there. People who are hungry or homeless, who lack medication and health care. And they just wander the squares. It's not much different from what we see in Third World countries. You have to remember that we deal with the poorest of the poor. There are people who still maintain some social security rights but that is not enough, as a poor woman-pensioner indicated. She said: "I buy either food or medicine. I can't buy both. The government's measures are now simply worsening."*

Panos Papanicolaou, Neurosurgeon: *"In all the countries 'supported' by the IMF, up to now, there has been a dramatic drop in average life expectancy. It's what we usually refer to as the average life span. There were countries where, after the IMF ordeal, the average life-span fell by 5-10 years. With the cuts we are facing now it's clear that our life expectancy will be greatly reduced. The citizens react. The government's response is in breach of even the basic principles of democracy. The penalization of wearing a hood, the unjustified arrests, and the hood-wearing policemen; all bordering on the para-state. This liberality with tear-gas leaves us no money for free education."*

Alain Badiou, Philosopher: ***"Crises are always solved through measures against society and against the people; which may be particularly harsh. This is how capitalism controls the situation. The problem of capitalism is how to get these measures accepted. For that, violence is deployed. In response to the 'financial gale alert', Democracy makes way of Debtocracy."***

[Aside Note: Real capitalism in the world has never been practiced. False capitalism is a wolf disguised as a sheep.]

DebtOcracy

4
DebtOcracy

A crisis of capitalism causes intensive devaluation. The value is lost through financial speculation. Somebody has to pay for this devaluation. However, the capitalists do not intend to pay for it. They're not at all altruistic [Altruism is regard for the interests of others].

But if those who caused the crisis do not intend to pay for it, why should we pay? In the past, dozens of countries have successfully repudiated debts not incurred by their citizens, in accordance with provisions of the international law, such as the concept of "odious debt".

The history of "odious debt": Our story starts in the 1920's with Alexander Sack. Sack was a minister and law specialist in Czarist Russia. After the 1917 Revolution, he taught in the universities of Europe and the USA. And in 1927, he came up with a brilliant concept, the concept of "odious debt".

To define a debt as odious, three requirements are needed.

1. The government of the country receives a loan without the knowledge and approval of the people.
2. The loan is spent on activities not beneficial to the people.
3. The lenders know this but play possum.

The United States of America had found themselves in need of the "odious debt" concept when they won the Spanish American War and annexed Cuba, in 1898.

Their problem was that, together with Cuba they acquired the debt incurred by the Spanish colonial regime. And, since Spanish colonialism had lasted for four-centuries, from 1492, when Columbus set foot in America, until 1898, that debt was quite great. Of course, the USA had no intention of paying for the mistakes of past regimes. They decided that Cuba's debt was odious and simply refused to pay it.

The same had happened in Mexico a few decades earlier, when the Republicans overthrew Emperor Maximilian I.

After they overthrew Emperor Maximilian I, they decided that the debt he had incurred was odious. Maximilian had borrowed huge sums at excessively high interest rates to deal with the uprising against him. And since he owed a lot, mainly to the people of Mexico, he was sentenced to death and sent to the firing squad.

In the late 19th and early 20th century, most instances of odious debt concerned under-developed countries on the American continent. Actually, a rising Super Power was involved in all those debt repudiations: The USA.

Sack's proposals sound progressive, even revolutionary.

Actually, at that time, his proposals served their interests; and this same Super Power brought the concept of odious debt into the 21st century.

5
US Attack On Iraq

December 2002: The White House is putting the finishing touches on the planned invasion and occupation of Iraq. Before the attack starts, however, American officials are preparing for the day; after Saddam Hussein's overthrow.

The State department knows that they will have to deal with Iraq's huge national debt. Therefore, they are trying to prove that this debt is odious.

Side-bar: *"The Interim government should seek a formal moratorium on debt service while coherent plans are prepared to deal with both Iraq's financing for its reconstruction and development."*

A secret task force is formed, and they propose that the first provisional government of Iraq declare cessation of due payments on the pretext that the Iraqi people must not pay the odious debt incurred by the Iraqi regime. All is now ready for the attack.

George Bush, then President of the United States: *"My fellow citizens . . . at this hour, American and coalition forces are in the early stages of military operations to disarm Iraq, to free the people, and defend the world from danger."*

Eric Toussaint, President of the Commission for the Abolition of Third World Debt: *"In March 2003, the USA and their allies invaded Iraq. Three weeks later, the US Secretary of the Treasury called for a summit meeting of*

G8 finance ministers, in Washington, and announced that Hussein's debt was odious. He said, 'Hussein's regime is a dictatorship and its debt must be repudiated. The new government of Iraq must be free of Hussein's debt."

George Bush, then President of the United States: *"Major combat operations in Iraq have ended and in the battle of Iraq the United States and its allies have prevailed."*

George Bush instructed former Secretary of State, James Baker. Baker claimed that Saddam Hussein wasted his people's money on building palaces and buying arms. Among other things, American diplomats proved that Iraq owed billons of dollars to France and Russia, for the purchase of Exocet missiles and fighter aircraft such as Mirage F1's and MiG's.

Actually, Hussein's war was not that different from what many Western leaders do. To the Arabs, Palaces are what the Olympic Games are to the West, a demonstration of economic and geopolitical dominance.

The American diplomats finally proved that Iraq's debt was odious and that the Iraqi people were not obliged to pay it. However, Washington suddenly realized that they'd pried open a can of worms. For the first time in the 21st century, the ultimate Super Power had legitimized the concept of "odious debt". So they chose to sweep this case under the rug.

The other countries said, "We'll cut 40% off Iraq's debt through the Paris Club". But the concept of odious debt must not be used, officially. Because other countries may claim this right as well.

For example, the DR Congo will repudiate Mobutu's debt. The Philippines will refuse to pay the debt of dictator Marcos, and South Africa will refuse the debt of the apartheid regime.

To prevent the extension of the concept of odious debt into the 21st century, they reached an ad hoc decision on Iraq. However, it is obvious to us, that the "odious debt doctrine" was used.

Barack Obama, President of the United States: *"I think it would be a mistake for Iraq to continue to be burdened by the sins of a deposed dictator."*

The USA continued to help Iraq to cancel old debts, but nobody in Washington ever wanted to hear again the expression "odious debt." [Ed. Can you blame them?]

Iraq managed to write off a big part off its debt with the support of an Empire.

But another country resolved to stand on its own two feet and stand up against the IMF, and its other lenders. They managed to prove that their debt was not only odious, but also illegitimate and unconstitutional.

Welcome Ecuador.

DebtOcracy

6
Concerning Ecuador

Rafael Correa, President of Ecuador: *"We have national commitments, more urgent than international ones. We will fulfill our international obligations as soon as we are able. But our priorities are clear. Life comes first, repaying debts second."*

Ecuador could have been one of the richest countries in South America. But from the moment oil was discovered all the country knew was dictators, poverty, debt, and economic hit-men.

John Perkins, Activist, former economic hit-man: *"My real job was deal making — giving loans to other countries. Huge loans. Much bigger than they could possibly repay. And one of the conditions of the loan — say of 1 billion dollars to a country like Indonesia or Ecuador — this country would then have to give 90% of that loan back to a US company, or US companies, to build their infrastructure. Halliburton or Bechtel, these were the big ones: And those companies would then go in and build electrical systems, ports, and highways. And these would basically serve just a few of the very wealthiest families in those countries. The poor people in those countries would then be stuck ultimately with this amazing debt that they could not possible repay."*

In 1982, Ecuador was visited by the IMF and a committee of wise men representing the countries big lenders.

Ecuador had been forced to borrow more and more, in order to fulfill past obligations.

Hugo Arias, Head of Ecuador audit Committee: *"Ecuador was constantly being looted by the countries of the North. For example, from 1980-1990 up to 2005 almost 50% of the government budget was used to repay debts. Namely about 3-4 billion US dollars a year! Only 4% was for health care. Four billion for repaying debts, 400 million for health care. We were killing our own people. The people of Ecuador protested. For a moment, things appeared to be under control, when Lucio Gutirrez took over. Gutirrez promised social benefits. He spoke like a socialist, but as soon as he took office he made a new deal with the IMF, and implemented measures of extreme austerity. The people decided that he should leave with the same means of transport favored by Argentinian presidents: the chopper."*

Vice President Papcio takes over. He has good intentions, but soon succumbs to Washington. So the people turn to the only politician who'd resist international pressure, Rafael Correa.

Song: *Una Sola Vuelta — From the first round. Correa, from the first round. Ecuador from the first round. Hope is triumphant. We are your united people. March on Ecuador Alliance. March on for Justice. March on for your rights. March on, Correa, for Ecuador. From the first round, Correa, from the first round. Ecuador from the first round.*

Carrea studied economics in Europe and the USA and knows very well how to handle the World Bank and the IMF — as long as one has the political will.

As Minister of France, in 2005, Correa declared that it was unnatural to use oil reserves in order to pay back the debt. This was unfair to the people. He said that 80% of the revenues should be used for health benefits, education and the creation of jobs, and only 20% should be channeled towards repayment of the debt. The World Bank said that they wouldn't lend to Ecuador if such a law passed. This was obvious interference with Ecuador's internal policy.

Correa declared that he would never follow such instructions from the World Bank. He chose to resign rather than succumb. This made him very popular. The people said: "This man chose to resign from the ministry, in order to defend the dignity and the interest of the people."

Correa was finally elected in 2006. One of his first actions was to deport the representatives of the World Bank and ask the IMF delegation to leave the Central Bank premises. Officials of the IMF, such as Bob Traa, who later came to Greece, had already been dubbed "unwanted" by the people of Ecuador.

Those callous, dishonest bureaucrats have to respect our country. This is why we deported the World Bank delegation. We maintain the right to restore the damage done to our country, and declare our debt to the World Bank illegitimate. Six months later Correa went a step further. He fulfilled the demands of social organizations for an audit committee.

Eric Toussaint, President of the Commission for the Abolition of Third World Debt: *"I was one of the people Correa chose for the Committee. 18 individuals and 4 national organizations participated. We were to examine all debt contracts from 1956 to 2006. We worked for 14 months. We examined the bond debt, the debts to the IMF, the WB, and other international organizations. We examined the debt to countries such as France, Japan, and Germany. Finally we examined Ecuador's internal national debt. The battle to access the data was tremendous. In the Ministry of Finance, our associate, Alejandro Olmos Jr. and myself, were declared persona non grata. The officials in the Ministry of Finance wrote to the Ministry to complain and denounce both mine and Olmos' actions claiming that we were inflicting harm on the Ministry's employees. We laughed it off, but you can imaging how difficult it was, after we'd been accused of being the bad guys in that procedure."*

Despite the setbacks, the Committee managed to complete its work and discovered that a big part of the debt was illegitimate. They acknowledged their findings to the state, who told the people. The work of the Committee was made public and this is very important.

The people of Ecuador now know why the debt contracts of past regimes, especially those of the year 2000, were illegitimate.

Song: *Dale Correa Rafael — March on, Rafael Correa. Our homeland is marching against the decadent Congress and the bureaucratic dictatorship of the old politicians. The people of Ecuador want a new Constitution. March on Correa. Correa, strike against the bosses who devastated our homeland. March on Correa. March on Rafael Correa.*

Based on the findings of the Committee, the government proved that the debt was illegitimate and declared cessation of payments for 70% of Ecuador's debt in bonds. Those in possession of Ecuador's debt had sold bonds at 20% of their value. They gave 800 million dollars and bought off 3 million dollars of debt. This significant reduction allowed an improvement in living conditions.

Furthermore, they rid themselves of the interest they would have had to pay till 2012 or 2030. They saved at least 7 billion dollars which was great for the country. This allowed the government to increase expenditures on health care, education, the creation of new jobs, and improvements in infrastructure.

Ecuador is no longer for sale.

7
Greece Again

In Greece, historians, economists and political analysis use up tons of ink daily to tell us how to handle our national debt. Yet there is one question very few pose. Do the Greek people really owe as much as their creditors claim? The debt incurred by Greece recently, fears evidence of illegitimacy. For example, the authorities received "gifts" from companies such a Siemens, who, together with Siemens Hellas, bribed ministers and officials for at least a decade, in order to gain contracts.

In this case, we have evidence of illegality and illegitimacy. So this debt should be examined in court.

Greek justice proved inadequate in the Siemens case. And it was too slow in other cases of deals made behind the people's back which have increased the debt.

With the infamous swaps of 2001, the government mortgaged the future to present a false prosperous present. They made the Greek debt look lower by changing a loan from JPY [Japan] to EUR [Europe] using outdated exchange rates. They were assisted in this by Goldman Sachs, who made millions out of this deal.

Mark Kirk, United States Senator: *"I am particularly concerned about the role of US financial institutions, particularly Goldman Sachs. As Greece got on the "heroine" of borrowed money, Goldman Sachs was the "crack dealer."*

The trick worked for many years. And the Greek political

elite showed they could reward their allies amply. They re-hired Goldman Sachs as consultant and paid them with the people's money.

Jean Quatremuer, Journalist, Liberation: *"Goldman Sachs consulted and attacked the Greek government, simultaneously."*

The scandal was revealed in 2010. A few days earlier, a former employee of Goldman Sachs had been assigned leader of the Greek Public Debt Management Agency.

Hiring an employee of GS is like hiring a criminal. It's the same as hiring a bank robber to guard your house. You think that he knows how robbers think so he'll be a better guard. But there's a great danger that one day he'll rob YOU and vanish. Who can guarantee that this former GS man will handle Greek affairs in the best possible way?

Several countries blame Greece for her transactions with Goldman Sachs. Only these are the same countries who exploit their liaisons with Greek governments, who sell weapons to Greece at a good price.

Sahra Wagenknecht, Deputy Chairperson, Die Linke: *"When, one year ago, Germany was negotiating to support Greece, one of the main terms was that Greece would continue to import German arms; Greece should cut down on pensions and social benefits, not on arms imports. This is indicative of the interests involved. Germany protects the interests of military equipment manufacturers, and its export industry. Those people want to continue trading despite the crisis."*

Daniel Cohn-Benit, President, European Greens-European Free Alliance: *"We're hypocrites! Last month, France sold 5 frigates to Greece for 2.5 billion dollars. Also helicopters worth 400 million and Rafael air-craft at 100 million each. I don't know if we sold 10, 20, or 30. The cost is almost 3 billion. Germany sold 6 submarines to Greece, worth 1 billion. We're such hypocrites! We give them money so they can buy our arms."*

Spirit of the Games

Before the hypocrisy of Europe, criminal backgrounds come hand-in-hand with criminal decisions always for "Greece's own good" or to support a new Greek expansionism that will lead to economic devastation.

Eric Toussaint, President of the Commission for the Abolition of Third World Debt: *"Here were huge expenses of the Olympic Games, and the cost now burdens the people. The loans for the Olympic Games were paid with tax-payer's money. It's only natural that the people demand to know why the budget exploded and where that money went."*

The Olympic Games and the corrupt transactions of Siemens or Goldman Sachs are but a small fraction of the shady deals made at the people's expense. However, there are more important matters which concern not only Greece, but all peripheral European countries.

Costas Lapavitsas, Professor of Economics: *"Have all the rules which govern the issuing of bonds been followed? Also, are there any questions of legitimacy about the banks who played the main role for issuing bonds either in the primary market or secondary market? Which banks took part? How were they reimbursed? Under what terms and conditions did they participate?"*

Sahra Wagenknecht, Deputy Chairperson, Die Linke: *"Part of the national debts incurred in Eurozone countries is illegitimate because they resulted from policies against the people's interest. So they must not be paid by the people."*

Ecuador demonstrated how all those illegitimate or odious contracts can come to light thorough an audit Committee. Why don't they tell us what kind of debt this is? How much is it? How was it incurred? To whom do we owe the money? This is why an audit is necessary. An audit will define exactly what this debt is about. We have to know and denounce all the lies told by the government and the corporations who seized the Greek people's money and all those who get amply paid to parrot and praise the government.

But who's going to setup the Audit Committee? And most of all, how can we make sure that it won't be yet another Parliament Committee consisting of the same people who got us into this situation?

The Audit Committee's members should not be specialists. It's not necessary. Because if the government forms a committee of specialists even if they are called from abroad, the committee may prove to be the government's mouthpiece.

Only the people have the authority and the right to request an audit because they suffer the consequences. All Greeks must become involved. All social organizations must protest and demand an audit.

The Greek political parties ND and PASOK who benefited from the creation of debt are very negative towards an audit, as their responsibility will be revealed. People, organizations, unions, judges, intellectuals, artists — everybody must act. They must express their views and exert pressure on political authority.

In March 2011, a group of people from different backgrounds took the initiative to demand the formation of an Audit Committee in Greece. Academics, writers, artists, union representatives from all over the world supported this initiative willingly. The Audit Committee will find which parts of the debt are odious or illegitimate and will prove, as provided by Greek and international law, that the Greek people are not obligated to pay such debt.

However, the decision is basically political, not financial. Even if the debt was legitimate, no government has the right to kill its people in order to satisfy its lenders.

Even if the entire Greek national debt of 350 billion proves legitimate, which is clearly not going to be the case, Greece can never pay it back. It will have to be cancelled. If honoring the debt and making it sustainable involves dismantling health care, dismantling education, dismantling the transportation systems, then the debt is socially unsustainable.

What in fact the government design is, that if they are going to default in relationship to the Greek people, I don't understand how a democratic socialist popularly elected government could turn to its own voters, and say we're going to default on YOU, instead of defaulting on the financial institutions.

Nobody is obliged to pay this debt, since it was accrued because of corruption in the financial markets. It's immoral to pay an immoral debt.

The formation of an Audit Committee is ultimately just a valuable weapon in a greater battle. This battle will follow the traditional rules by which battles have been fought for centuries. Without this battle, even if we repudiate the debt repeatedly, it will always rise from its ashes.

This means that a field for ideological, political, and class struggle will form. The debt is a result of class struggle.

Don't hesitate to stand up for you rights against the EU and the Greek government. Respect is gained through struggle; not by obeying one's creditor.

Look at Tunisia and Egypt. Only when the people take action can the situation really change.

We have to shake off submissiveness, liberate ourselves from the IMF, liberate ourselves from the European Central Bank, and liberate ourselves from the European Union, because all three mean the economic slavery of Greece.

Giorgos Papidreou: Prime Minister of Greece: *"**Now is the critical moment. Let's go!***

DebtOcracy (2011)
with Englilsh Subs 1:14:48
http://tinyurl.com/43nx2mg

We Americans *also* have to shake off submissiveness. And liberate ourselves from The United Nations, liberate ourselves from The United States, Inc., and liberate ourselves from the non-federal Federal Reserve Bank, because all three mean the economic slavery of America.

Support The Republic for the united States of America instead.

http://republicfortheunitedstates.org/

DebtOcracy

8

National Debt Free 'Money'

Chapter 1 from
Give Yourself Credit: Money Doesn't Grow On Trees

There is no reason for us to put up with recession, depression, and unemployment.

By using 2006 figures, we see that Americans payed out about $14 trillion dollars to produce services and goods (GNP) for which they earned back about $10 trillion dollars of income (GNI), about $1 trillion dollars of which was reinvested in the economy, leaving about $9 trillion dollars of income earned to cover the about $14 trillion dollars cost of the services and goods that they consumed.

In other words, the **available purchasing power** of the United States was only about $9 trillion dollars, or about $5 trillion dollars less than the **total collective cost of services and goods purchased and consumed**. Now, where did the consumers get the additional $5 trillion dollars that they spent on services and goods? They borrowed it from the banks that **created it out of nothing as credit,** by simple accounting entries on their books.

If the government were to replace this **interest bearing 'bank-created-out-of-nothing' credit** with **non-interest bearing 'government-created-out-of-nothing' credit** instead — the total money supply would remain unchanged and a whopping $5 trillion dollars **of new government issued national interest-free credit** would be fed into the economy, without increasing either the rate of inflation or the federal national debt, and this **new government issued national interest-free credit** could be used to pay a guaranteed monthly dividend to all Americans — such as $10,000 per adult and $5,000 for each dependent child — **instead of GIVING needless interest to the private non-federal Federal Reserve banks.**

If $5 trillion dollars of **freely created national debt-free credit** were issued to fill the gap between our production costs (GNP) and our purchasing power (GNI), and if this $5 trillion dollars of **new national debt-free credit** were distributed among the people, in monthly dividends, the government would still have more than $1 trillion dollars each year to satisfy its budgetary needs, without a federal income tax.

By utilizing **new national debt-free credit,** Congress could stabilize prices, — and output would increase to full employment!

In other words, there is no reason for us to put up with recession, depression and unemployment. The government simply has **to put more 'money' into circulation.**

It can all be paid for if the government increased the 'money supply' by **issuing national debt-free credit,** as Abe Lincoln did at the start of the Civil War.

We suffer from a **failure of consumer demand** because of consumer's lack of buying power — because of our failure to use **our God-given national debt-free credit** to prime the pump.

Our country was pulled out of the Depression by priming the pump with liquidity that put **new 'money'** into the people's pockets.

Watering a liquidity starved economy with **new national debt-free credit** — instead of **borrowing credit at interest** from the banks **and then PAYING it back to the banks** — would work wonders.

People want to work, and there is work to be done.

Consumers want to purchase the fruits of their labor, but they can't, because of the anemic money supply. An infusion of **new national debt-free credit** — instead of borrowing more interest laden debt from the banks — would get the wheels of production turning again!

Very little **borrowed 'money'** goes to improve infrastructure or to increase employment. Jobs are being out-sourced abroad while the public struggles to make the interest payments on the **needless federal debt** — and stay alive.

DebtOcracy

9
Dispense With Deflation

Deflation is a *shortage of the people's buying power* relative to *the power of the nation to produce.* But when production is cut-down, as usually happens in a depression, then workers lose their jobs and the people's buying power is still further reduced, relative to the power of the nation to produce.

The country and the people get progressively poorer, and nobody profits except the people who either have hoarded money, or the people who have the power to create it in the first place, such as the banks. For all they have to do is sit on their money, or their power to create it, and watch the price of everything go down, to their advantage, which means that the purchasing power of their withheld money goes up correspondingly.

"Depression" is another word for "Deflation". Depressions are never caused by *"over-production".* They are caused by *"under consumption"* which is, in turn, caused by *a lack of buying power* in the hands of would be consumers.

So the only thing to do when faced with Deflation is to *increase the buying power* of the people.

The first thing that is needed is the creation of *an additional supply of new 'money'* in such a way as to NOT increase debt — made available to the masses of the people so that they can purchase the services and goods which producers are eager and needing to produce and sell.

To put the matter simply, the general thing that is needed, when deflation threatens — as like now — is to have Congress or its appointed agency create the proper amount *of national debt-free 'money',* or *debt-free credit,* on the Treasury books, and use it to expand the present monetary system into a national program that will *put active buying power* directly into the hands of the people who will spend it for the general good.

There is simply no good reason why the people of this nation should be called upon to suffer through another period of Deflation and business stagnation. *Not if Congress does its constitutional duty* as we must insist.

There is no need to fear inflation as long as our national productive capacity is not exceeding its 100 percent capacity to produce.

10
Good Times and Bad

That which happened to America, after the Stock Market crash of 1929, was something like what happened to America in 1896, when disappointed seekers after homestead land started to trek back east, having found that the last good prairie land was gone and that the lands they had tried to farm could not sustain their families.

For two and a half centuries Americans had taken completely for granted that they could move west and make a new start whenever they needed or wanted to.

These dejected land seekers coming back east symbolized *the end of an epoch* for the common folks.

So at the close of 1929, and in 1930, America faced for the first time the fact that *her old methods* of achieving economic and industrial expansion could not continue forever, any more than her people's search for fertile farmlands in the west.

Another great American epoch had come to an end.

So *when the "New Deal" was born* under Franklin Delano Roosevelt, we reacted according to the law of self-preservation because we instinctively knew that *times like those of the past were gone, and were never coming back* because of the increasing division of labor, the increasing inter-dependence of the people, and the complete absence of a free land frontier.

The tremendous obstacles to people of little means, in surviving the Great Depression and starting over again, meant that the country could not again stand a period *when the government just stood by and watched the credit structure collapse.*

Periods of bankruptcy were the price that had to be paid for the government letting the economic life of the country alone, no matter come what may. For under the debt-laden money system that we have today, *periods of "boom"* brought about by the credit expansion of private banks *must always be followed by periods of unemployment and depression.*

When credit contraction takes place, and unsupportable debt burdens are allowed to collapse and be written off in bankruptcy, economic hopelessness and loss affect millions of people and many businesses too.

The ancient Hebrews had a better way. Every seven years they cancelled all debt and started over freshly anew. The farmers didn't have to give up their farms and families didn't have to give up their homes. So their system worked very well.

Only by using the most illogical and utterly unsound measures *can industrial expansion be supported today under the debt monetary and financial system we use.*

Some of those illogical and unsound methods of attempting to make the economic system of today "add up" have already been tried.

Only at times, when a net addition to the purchasing power of the people, over and above that paid out by industry, has there been full employment and prosperity in recent times. For *industry never distributes enough buying power* to enable the people to buy the increasing amount of goods that it can and does produce.

Modern industries can *increase their output of goods*

without any corresponding *increase in the amount of money they pay out* in wages, interest, rent, or dividends, into the hands of consumers.

So something else has to happen *to make up for this deficiency of consumer buying power* — or the goods industries produced can't be sold.

War is one of the illogical and certainly tragic and wasteful ways the economic system can be gotten to "add up."

During a war the government borrows a lot of money from the banks, at interest, and spends in on armaments and troops. *Armaments are something the people can't buy, though they receive wages for producing it.* And all other industries gain this *additional buying power* to add to what they pay out themselves. It keeps them going by giving them a dependable market for which to produce.

Of course the cost of war requires a tremendous addition to the National Debt.

But War wasn't the only thing *that kept our industries going* in pre- "New Deal" times.

During the 1920's, *America gave away,* up until the Depression, *about $22 billion dollars worth of goods!* That is, we produced them and shipped them abroad and never got paid for them. We gave foreigners *buying power* over American goods. This was one way of *"developing a market."* Part of it was the result of the sales, in the United States, of *worthless foreign bonds* during the 1920's.

Also, state and local governments *increased their indebtedness* by $10 trillions dollars and spent it into the hands of the people who in turn spent it into the economy for services and goods.

And during the 1920's, *consumers went into deb*t buying goods on *the installment plan,* to the amount of another $10 trillion dollars by, 1929. Americans *took off of the market* more goods than they had money in hand to pay for at the time.

These were some of the *stop-gaps* that made it *appear that all was well,* and gave a false sense of security to the American people until the crash of 1929. *But the crash did come.* That depression seemed more like an abyss than a depression.

For example: We became afraid that machines were going to take more and more jobs away from the people. With monopolies at work and *with a debt money system that only produced buying power by increasing debt,* machine production was always *decreasing the buying power of consumers.*

Machines *would not create unemployment* if so many of the machines were not controlled by monopolistic combinations and concerns. Monopolies and machines, and technical improvements cause unemployment *because monopolies maintain high prices to restrict output.* Monopolies siphon the benefits of the machines *off into corporate surpluses* made possible by very excess profits.

Under true competition, *the benefits of the machines would go to consumers* in lower prices *and to the producers too,* instead of to the banks, *because consumers would have greater purchasing power than before.*

The Anti-Trust Division of the Justice Department and the Tennessee Valley Authority had the effect of breaking down monopoly price structures and reducing the cost of goods and services to consumers.

Between 1922 and 1929, the output per worker in the United States increased by 18%.

Therefore, one of three things had to happen. Either . . .

1. the people would have to buy 18% more goods at reduced prices; or

2. 18% more money had to be created and put into the hands of the people; or

3. 18% of the workers would have to be discharged.

Unless **one of the first two things** were done, it would be necessary to fire workers because **industry was producing as much as it had before** but with fewer workers.

Monopoly control of Industry prevents a reduction of prices. And **monopoly control of Finance** prevents an increase in the volume of money. So the third thing happens: **the people lose their jobs.**

A general reduction of prices has never happened before in a free economy. Never has there been a period of prosperity when the price level was going down. Furthermore, over a long period of time, wages constantly continue to rise.

In other words, **the answer** to machines and increased efficiency **is increased buying power** for the common man instead of the banks.

The central question is, then, shall the additional money needed to supply this **necessary increase in buying power** be provided by the government creating the additional money needed interest free? Or must **increasing debt bring collapse and depression** in its wake?

If the buying power of the dollar is kept at a constant level, and if the people as a whole through their Congress exercise **their constitutional power to create money interest free,** then **monopolies** and **the destitutions upon true economic liberty will be removed.**

No power on earth makes monopoly control of real wealth *so easy to achieve* as the power of private banks to create money out of thin air and expand it at interest.

Had the big city banks not been able to create their money *by ink marks on paper out of thin air,* it would have been much more difficult *for competing firms to be bought out,* or for their control *to be taken over by financial Concerns.*

And nothing has contributed as much to the destruction of small scale business as decreases in the purchasing power of the dollar. It has always been at such times *that farmers have lost their farms and banks and insurance companies have become landlords, and little businesses have gone under,* leaving their financially empowered competitors to control an even greater share of the market, when the cycle turns upward again.

By 1929 one-third of our people could produce all of the necessities of life needed by all the people. And unless all the people were able to consume their share of the necessities, even that one-third couldn't keep their jobs, hence the Great Depression.

What those businessmen needed was *more demand for the goods that they had the capacity to produce and sell.* But under the debt-money system we have today, *the only way buying power can be increased* is by expansion of someone's debt. Almost all of our money is created by the banks *writing up demand deposits out of thin air* and using them to make interest bearing loans.

But debt expansion cannot go on forever.

Sooner or later debt has to be forgiven, repudiated, or paid.

11
The Deluge of Debt

The old Biblical tale of Noah and the Flood has its modern parallel in the world's red ink.

We are told that in Noah's day the world was submerged under great waters. But our modern flood of red ink is even greater than Noah's flood and is just as real. For in our day we are steadily sinking under a deluge of debt.

We are not thinking of War Debts, or of International Debts, or of any correlatives of these which may be in the limelight at any given moment, but of the system itself by which *all money is debt repayable to the banks.*

Struggle against this as we may, so long as money comes into being as a debt repayable to the banks, we are their slaves. As Colbourne says, Even our vocabulary is perverted. When a bank is said to extend you **"credit"** it is doing nothing of the kind; it is extending you **"debt"**.

It may be a disturbing thought to realize that *the bulk of our money is debt-money created by the banks* on the basis of the country's resources and its ability to deliver wanted goods. But however disturbing this may be, it is nevertheless true. *Our money is circulating evidence of debt repayable to the banks.* This is the solid fact which we must grasp:

The bulk of our money is Debt-Money repayable to the non-federal Federal Reserve Bank.

UNPAYABLE DEBT

Is it any wonder that we sink in a flood of debt when every article of wealth we buy must be paid for with money which itself is debt? Debt surrounds us from birth to the grave. We cannot be rid of its grip because of the ingenious financially invented device called INTEREST.

Odious INTEREST Denounced

The deluge of our present debt can never be drained away because *interest requires that the debtor repay more than has been loaned to him.* The process by which Debt-Money is created is cumulative — it grows. The debt cannot be liquidated because it grows faster than business can repay it. *Debt can never be repaid, now or at any other time.*

Thomas A. Edison is authority for the statement, *"In all our great bond issues the interest is always greater than the principal."* The total of principal and interest, which is more than the original loan, can be met only by *the creation of more new fresh debt to cover the interest.* Thus debt breeds more debt, and the more we struggle the deeper we sink.

And our situation, bad as it appears now, is growing worse. For example, when we try to use this borrowed money to utilize wealth from the shops of the nation *it becomes impossible, at the same time, to use the money to both utilize wealth from the shops, and repay the debt.* If we borrow $5.00 to buy a pair of shoes, we have to choose between buying the pair of shoes and repaying the debt. If we choose to buy the shoes, we still owe the debt of $5.00. We can either have the shoes or pay the debt but we can't do both at once.

But this is not the whole story. Business depends upon the debt-money of the banking system. Every dollar loaned to business must be recovered in prices. Now, money is never borrowed except to be spent; but, as it must subsequently be repaid, the borrowers have to spend it in producing, or inducing the production of something that can be sold; which means that **the harder the community works and the more it produces, the deeper it goes into debt to the banks.** So debt increases at the expense of our ability to buy goods.

It must, I think, be quite obvious to anybody that, if the world as a whole is consistently getting further and further into debt, **it is not,** as the ordinary business man would say, **"paying its way".** The public is paying all that it can and buying what it can. Its failure to pay more is therefore forcing the destruction of potential production and is at the same time piling up more debt.

How fast does debt grow? **In the 17th century** (*that is to say, in the century in which the Bank of England was founded*) **the world debt** (*and we have plenty of accurate figures with regard to these matters*) **increased 47%.** The Bank of England was founded at the end of the 17th century.

By the end of the 18th century **the world debt** had **increased by 466%,** and by the end of the 19th century the world debt, public and private, had **increased by 12,000%.** And, according to some very exact calculations which have been carried out by a quite irreproachable professor of industrial engineering of Columbia University, Professor Rautenstrauch, taking the year 1800 as the origin and taking one hundred years as the unit, **the world debt is now increasing as the 'fourth power' of time;** that is to say, increasing as time goes on, not as the square of time and

not as the cube of time, *but as the 'fourth power' of time.*
And that is in spite of the numerous repudiations of debt,
which take place with every bankruptcy and other methods
to write off debts and start again.

The Key to Deliverance from Debt:
But we must not miss *the one vital point* which gives
the Key to this dilemma. The Debt-Money created and
destroyed by banks is called **"financial-credit"** and in this
term, the word **"financial"** deserves our attention. It should
be"people-credit" instead.

The deluge of debt is purely **"financial debt"** since it is
based upon what the banks call *the "credit" that they
create.*

*A money system built on debt and interest can
function only to create more debt.* And this is precisely
what has happened. The facts of experience confirm our
findings. *Under this system, a shortage of money is
guaranteed.*

*The money system should be built on the credit of
the people on the land, instead of on interest and debt,*

12
The Bankers' Manifesto (1892)

The Banker's Manifesto was exposed by US Congressman Charles A. Lindbergh, Sr. (Minnesota), during his term of office (1907-17) as a warning to the citizens of America.

The Father and his famous son, Charles, Jr.

— — —

The Bankers' Manifesto

"We [the bankers] must proceed with caution and guard every move made, for the ***lower order of people*** are already showing signs of restless commotion. Prudence will therefore show a policy of apparently yielding to the popular will until our plans are so far consummated that we can de-

"At the coming Omaha Convention to be held July 4th [1892], our men must attend and direct its movement, or else there will be set on foot such antagonism to our designs as may require force to overcome. This at the present time would be premature. We are not yet ready for such a crisis. Capital must protect itself in every possible manner through combination [conspiracy] and legislation.

"The courts must be called to our aid, debts must be collected, bonds and mortgages foreclosed, as rapidly as possible.

"When through the process of the law, the common people have lost their homes, they will be more tractable and easily governed through the influence of the strong arm of the government applied to a central power of imperial wealth under the control of the leading financiers. People without homes will not quarrel with their leaders.

"History repeats itself in regular cycles. This truth is well known among our principal men who are engaged in *forming an imperialism of the world.* While they are doing this, the people must be kept in a state of political antagonism.

"The question of tariff reform must be urged through the organization known as the Democratic Party, and the question of protection with the reciprocity must be forced into view through the Republican Party.

"By thusly dividing voters, we can get them to expand their energies in fighting over questions of no importance to us, except as teachers to the common herd. Thus, by discrete action, we can secure all that has been so generously planned and successfully accomplished."

The dictatorship of the bankers and their debt-money system are not limited to one country, but exist in every country in the world. They are working to keep their control tight, since *one country freeing itself from this dictatorship and issuing its own interest- and debt-free currency,* setting the example of what an honest system could be, *would be enough to bring about the worldwide collapse of the bankers' swindling debt-money system.*

DebtOcracy

13
Consider This

When war broke out in 1939, the Government, which had been short of money for the past ten years, went to the banks to take out a first loan of $200 million dollars.

The banks did not have any more money on that day, than they had the day before. For the past ten years, the population had been lacking money. When one is lacking money, one hardly has any surplus to store in the bank.

Nevertheless, the banks loaned $200 million dollars to the Government that day. *They wrote $200 million dollars to the Government's credit in bookkeeping money.*

And the young people, who had been wandering about aimlessly for years because there was no money, were called immediately into action by the Government, dressed from head to toe in the Government's finest uniforms, lodged, fed, equipped, and transported to Europe to take part in the Slaughter of their Peers.

And this was seen in all the countries of the world.

The world had suffered from unemployment for ten years due to the world's scarcity of money. *Yet this same world was able to fight a very costly war.* Because the banks created all the bookkeeping money that was needed to finance that war.

Money for War! *No-money for Peace . . .*

DebtOcracy

14

Real Wealth Production

Chapter 4 from
Give Yourself Credit: Money Doesn't Grow On Trees

The limiting factor in the production of real wealth has been the failure to distribute to **would-be-consumers** enough money to buy the **potential output** of the producers of services and goods.

If the distribution of the **purchasing power** necessary to enable the nation to **consume their total production,** were made, they could equally consume **the goods of other nations as well,** which they might exchange for their production.

Any nation can safely **credit itself** with new-money-income and **pay it into active circulation** up to a certain easily determined total amount. That amount is the number of new dollars that can be put into circulation without prices increasing. The danger of inflation comes **only when too much money** is being put into circulation relative to the supply of goods. Therefore inflation and deflation menace a nation **only when the nation has inadequate control** over the creation and retirement **of its circulating media of exchange.**

Paying off portions of the federal National Debt can counter inflation any time it threatens, if those payments are properly employed.

And Deflation — the worst menace to the common people of limited means — could be prevented **according to a mandate of a caring Congress,** if a governmental authority, exclusively responsible for the creation of 'new money' and 'national credit', promptly placed in circulation **enough new purchasing power** to check any decline in the price of goods.

We will not have Inflation or Deflation if these things are done.

But with the private banks having **the power to create or destroy** money at will, through their technique of **odious fractional reserve banking,** Inflation and Deflation will alternately **plague the people, both off and on,** as it is doing and has done in the past, over the years.

The thing that leads to dangerous Inflation is not the creation of money by government, but **a continuous increase in public debt.** For whenever an interest-bearing debt becomes so large that its servicing requires a major portion of tax revenue **so large that the people lose hope of ever being able to pay it off,** then comes the temptation to reduce or eliminate the debt **by unsound, unjust, artificial means** — such as **by needless War.**

Then Inflation comes in, in earnest, not as an accident or a consequence of other factors, but **as a deliberate policy of a distressed people.**

While **needless war** is going on there are other costs that concern the people far more than financial ones or the soaring National Debt: **namely, the loss of lives most of all.**

The most important thing about war-finance, and tomorrows money, is that **other methods become known and put into effect** whereby the people can **escape the ever-mounting interest charges of the banks** by EARNING THEIR WAY out from under the debt that war leaves behind in its wake.

Under a *scientific, interest-free, monetary system* any people can and will *earn their way out of debt* if they *increase their national production* of services and goods.

And so we come to the final and truly hopeful point. A *scientific, interest-free monetary system* requires the *rate of increase* of money in circulation to be the same as the *rate of increase* of the production of goods.

And this increase of revenue *must not come from taxes or borrowing* which add to the National Debt. This increase of revenue *must consist of new interest-free 'money'*, created by the *issuing authority of the people's Congress* where its validity and buying power have *already been secured* by the prior production of the things for which this revenue has already been used to buy — hence the established principle of *"mutual offset credit exemption exchange"* [to follow].

The American people *can earn their way out of the National Debt* under the sort of scientific interest-free monetary system described in the author's book: "*Give Yourself Credit: Money Doesn't Grow On Trees."*

DebtOcracy

15
Shelter, Clothing & Food

The war that broke out upon the world, in September, 1939, was not just the Second World War. Not only was it a clash between one group of nations and another group, it was a world-wide struggle between two fundamentally different systems of government and philosophies of human life. The real victory is yet to be won or lost, not only by military might, but by enlisting the profound allegiance of the peoples of the world to one system or the other — the fight to the death between the slave world and the free.

The "four freedoms" enunciated by President Franklin Delano Roosevelt in his message to Congress, on January 6, 1941, are the very core of the revolution for which the United Nations have taken their stand.

We who live in the United States might think that there is nothing revolutionary about **Freedom of religion, Freedom of expression,** and **Freedom from the fear of secret police,** but when we think about the significance of **Freedom from want for the common man,** we see that the revolution of the past 200 years has not as yet been won, either here in the United States or in any other nation of the world. And we know that this revolution cannot stop until **Freedom from want** has eventually actually been attained. Those who **write the peace** must think of the whole world. We ourselves here in the United States are no more a master race than were the Nazis of Roosevelt's time.

Waging war **with our neighbors in the world** cannot but be a part of a profound transformation of the lives of all men and women around the world — for good or ill.

The forces of revolution and change derive their power from the bafflement and confusion of the age.

Why should men be unemployed when they themselves need the things they can and want to produce?

Why should people go hungry while farmers lose their land because they cannot sell their crops for a living price?

Why, indeed, should there be a depression and unemployment when producers want to work and when consumers are in dire need of the things the producers want to and could make available and sell today?

Why should "deflation" and "scarcity of money" stand in the way of fulfilling these fundamental human needs?

These old and threadbare questions lie at the root of the unrest that is rocking and shaking the world.

Ever since the beginning there have been these things that men have sought after. The first has been **food, warmth, and shelter:** the basic necessities of life. The second has been **security, or safety, and freedom from fear**. And the third has been **liberty of spirit: the right to call one's soul one's own**. And as man has progressed from age to age men have tended to value more and more the third of these things: **liberty of spirit**.

But with the coming of the industrial revolution the direct connection between man's labor and the supplying of his physical needs was broken. The division of labor into specialized tasks has practically destroyed the relationship that once existed between daily work and the production of man's own shelter, clothing, and food. **Thus unemployment appeared.**

Not for long can people tolerate a situation where they are told that they cannot work because there is no "demand" for their labor when at the same time they find their families in want. For they will say: "But there is a demand for us to work; there is a demand that we produce *shelter, clothing, and food.* For our families demand and need these things."

And while all this is true, they will be told, nevertheless, that "enough has already been produced." To which the people reply: "Then why can't we satisfy our families needs?"

But the wise ones will say, "But you have no money."

And to that the reply, should be: "Then give us the money and we will consume the surplus goods, and then there will be jobs for us and work for us to do."

And to this the answer comes: "But that would make you objects of government charity. It is better for you to remain unemployed" (**and on welfare instead**).

Not for long will men endure the utter foolishness of such answers to their questions. So dictators arise who tell the people that they will trade them jobs for the right to rule over them for all time. Thereby men have been forced by need-less circumstances to give up the third great and most valu-able objective of their search — **liberty of spirit** — in order, as they have been led to believe, that they might gain the first — *food, and the other necessities of life for their fami-lies and themselves* — purchased at the price of freedom and liberty.

So we become determined, therefore, to find a way in which the tragic conundrum or paradox of needless unem-ployment can be overcome without the loss of political or economic freedom. We must provide for full employment after the physical wars have been won.

The National Debt *does* matter. Policies cannot be pursued indefinitely by deficit spending. Even though — as it has been said — we owe the debt to ourselves, to our own people, what is paid in interest becomes income to someone else — **the creators and lenders of debt**. Though all the people must pay it, it is owed to a comparative few.

The servicing of the debt will require the payment of billions upon billions of needless dollars in taxes by every family, rich or poor, in the whole country. The larger the interest-bearing National Debt, the greater will be the problem of securing the distribution of buying power among the people to make full production and full employment possible. So the road to an ever-increasing National Debt is a road that leads to an economy more and more centralized in the hands of the few.

There is a limit to the proportion of its income that any nation can afford to pay **in needless interest** to the holders of its bonds. There is a limit to the tax burden that the American people can and will willingly bear.

No political party or group can expect to hold the support of the American electorate unless it can furnish that electorate some answer other than oratory to the problems of unemployment and the public debt. There must be jobs for returning soldiers and there must be full employment and opportunity for abundant consumption for all after war if we would protect our liberties with something other than constant "deficit financing" by government "borrowing-at-interest" of privately created credit and a consequent increase in the National Debt **that-ought-not-to-be-debt**.

There must be a better, sounder, more solid basis for full employment and an equally abundant economy than we have as yet laid down. Full employment, abundant production and equally abundant consumption can be achieved without economic dictatorship or government control of our economy. The job of government must be the motivation of full employment and production — in peacetime as well as in war — by government regularly passing its power on into the hands of the people of the nation.

The first line of economic defense should be to make certain that American consumers will have a constant buying power large enough in total volume to keep our machinery of productions going at a high enough level to provide employment to everyone who wants to and needs to work.

The more the products of a nation, such as the United States, it can ship away to other lands the better off it is. A **scientific, interest-free monetary system** such as this book describes would guarantee to its people, as a whole, the constant ability to consume as much and more than they could produce. This guarantee would remove the fear of imports which would bless a nation living under the false delusion that an abundance of goods causes unemployment and that unemployment is to be cured by reducing the supply of goods and services, instead of increasing effective demand.

The price of enduring peace is, first of all, the removal from the path of international trade the barrier of **uncollectible and needless debt,** by founding trade upon the principle of an equal exchange of services and goods among and between the peoples of the world.

Only when the domestic seller and foreign seller can be sure when he is paid in dollars that he is receiving money that will constantly buy the same quantity of American goods from year to year, will we have a rock upon which to build a trade that will make for a lasting peace and supply the world with the necessities of life.

DebtOcracy

16
Money Without Debt

The money system of the Roman Republic was a money system created without debt.

Rome became Mistress of the commerce of the world without the use of silver or gold. Her people were the bravest, and the most prosperous people, who knew no grinding poverty. *Her money was issued directly by the government* [not by banks], and was composed of a cheap material — copper and brass — based alone *upon the faith and credit of the people of Rome.*

With this *abundant money supply* she built her magnificent temples and courts and other public structures. She distributed her lands among the people in small holdings, and wealth poured into the coffers and treasury of Rome.

But, then, Julius Caesar drastically reduced the money supply. He began making gold coins with his image on them and declared himself Emperor of Rome for life, putting an end to Rome's *great experiment in elected government* called a Republic.

Gold coins have ever since been the money of the rich.

The representatives in the Senate hated gold money and the plutocracy (rule by the rich) that gold money implies.

Although the Senate assassinated Julius Caesar, *gold money had now taken root* supported by the very rich and the dictators they were able to buy with their gold.

After Julius Caesar was assassinated, copper and brass coins were removed from circulation and **the quantity of available money** was reduced by 90%!

A deep depression set in, **like today.** The average person had to sell his property in order to just buy the necessities of life. **The wealth of the nation was thereby quickly consolidated in the hands of the wealthiest Romans once again.** Gone was the incentive for the common good.

Then Rome was sacked by the Visigoths and humanity was plunged into the Dark Ages.

With cheap government issued money the Roman Republic flourished, but **with gold money it perished.**

This controversy between cheap money and gold money continues throughout history and is symbolized in part by the yellow brick road in the Wizard of Oz.

In England in 1100 A.D. there were no banks like we have today. The Goldsmiths controlled the economy of the nation and even the English Monarchy. By acting together, the Goldsmiths could either make money plentiful or scarce.

When they **made gold money plentiful,** the nation's economy flourished. But when they **made gold money scarce,** depression set in **and they could buy up the assets of the people for pennies on the dollar.**

About 1000 A.D. King Henry I, the son of England's first Norman King, William the Conqueror, was low on gold. A series of costly wars had depleted the treasury, so Henry **created a unique form of government money called tally sticks** — polished sticks of wood (usually hazel wood) **issued** by the government, by the king, **for the payment of taxes.** This made wooden tally sticks just as good as any other form of money for the payment of debts.

This effective **debt free money system** lasted for almost seven hundred years!

Without needless debt, England flourished into the greatest power on earth for centuries. **At its peak more than 95% of England's money was in the form of tally sticks.** Today, the only form of debt free government issued money is in the form of coins. About 3% in the United Kingdom, and far less in the United States.

After **democratizing** the money power with tally sticks, King Henry **democratized** political power itself. Then came **the Charter of Liberties** — followed by **the Magna Charta** in 1215.

A merchant class began to develope.

The first Parliamentarian elections were held in 1265. **Government by the people of England was born,** and in 1600, serfdom was legally banned. Humanity in England was finally set free.

Simple sticks of wood broke the debt money system in England for almost seven hundred years! (1000 A.D.-1694)

Then the Bank of England was founded, in 1694.

Every dollar in circulation in America today is an interest bearing debt created by the government by **selling interest bearing bonds** [IOUs] [promissory notes] [promiises to pay] to the private non-federal Federal Reserve Bank.

Americans are being robbed blind and they don't even know who's doing the robbing. The problem that's driving the economy into the ground is **needless debt** supported and **allowed by the Congress and the people of the United States!**

When government spends more than it collects in taxes, it is **self-forced to borrow the difference** by selling interest bearing IOUs, to the private non-federal Federal Reserve Bank **that pays for them with the "Credit" of we the people of the United States.**

When a US bank sells a $100 US interest bearing bond to the private non-federal Federal Reserve Bank, the bank gets **to loan out ten times that amount,** so the bank not only gets back **the $100 plus interest for the bond** from the Federal Government, **it gets back an additional $1000 plus interest that it created in loans to other borrowers, based on the "Credit" of we the people of the United States.**

($100 at 5% interest = $105 x 10 more = 11 x $105 = $1155 total [out of thin air] = 1155% interest on a $100 sale).

The bank is making more than 1100% interest on that simple $100 deposit to the bank!

This is why bank buildings are among the biggest buildings on the planet.

This system of **lending what you do not have** is called Fractional Reserve lending (FRL).

All of our money is created by banks lending **'money' created out of thin air** to people, companies, and the government — when the government could simply issue its money debt-free — instead of borrowing it at interest from the non-federal Federal Reserve Bank.

By simply issue it itself money debt-free equally for the benefit of we the people of the United States. Abraham Lincoln did it and others did it. **But the government is in partnership with the private non-federal Federal Reserve Bank!**

"In our debt money system someone has to borrow every dollar we have in circulation. If the banks create ample money we are prosperous; if not, we starve. When one gets a complete grasp of the picture, the tragic absurdity of our hopeless position will be seen as incredible. It is the most important subject intelligent persons can investigate and reflect upon." — 1934, Robert H. Hemphill, Credit Manager of the Federal Reserve Bank of Atlanta.

The government doesn't need to go into debt, it can issue all the money it needs, itself.

What government officials can't raise from taxes, they now borrow from banks.

An Oligarchy is a group of powerful people **who have hijacked the United States Government** by going into partnership with the private non-federal Federal Reserve Bank.

You can't borrow yourself out of debt. No one is talking about the debt system that enslaves the people.

The government should take charge of the money supply. All that matters is who controls the QUANTITY" of the money supply.

DebtOcracy

17
We The People Provide The Credit

"No state shall...make any __thing__ but gold and silver coin a tender in payment of debts..." — Art. 1, Sec. 10, clause 1 of the Constitution **FOR** the United States of America, and the CONSTITUTION **OF** THE UNITED STATES, INC.

In order to circumvent this constitutional rule and in order to make paper Federal Reserve Notes (FRNs) *"a tender in payment of debts",* Congress turned to its *"power...to borrow money on the credit (of we the people) of the United States."* — Art. 1, Sec. 10, clause 1.

Since Congress borrows "money substitutes" (FRNS) on the basis of *my credit* since I am one of the people of the United States, Congress gives *me* an unlimited *credit exemption* that I can use to discharge the debts that I cannot **"pay"** with FRN's, because FRNs are not **real** *"money of account of the United States"* that **"pays"** debts. Congress permits me to use my *personal credit exemption* to **"pay"** charges that Federal Reserve Notes can only **"discharge."**

Part four of the 1040 ES booklet under "Estimated Tax Worksheet" in reference to *"exemptions",* says: *"If you can be claimed as a dependent on another person's return your 'personal exemption' is NOT allowed."*

This is saying in effect that *my* personal exemption *IS allowed* if I am not claimed as a dependent on another *"persons"* (*corporation's*) return. In other words, the industrial society will claim my *personal exemption — my mutual offset credit exemption exchange* — if I don't claim it myself.

The above declaration is a *second witness* to my **REMEDY** for being an *accommodating party* to the corporate UNITED STATES via my *pledge of credit* to the public debt. I am claiming the UNITED STATES as my dependant because I am *accommodating the UNITED STATES* with my pledge of personal credit to the public debt.

We the people are the source of the *commercial energy* that our credit represents.

We the people provide the credit for every instrument that we endorse, the very instant we endorsed it with our credit sign.

Our signature represents the intangible personal credit that we provide. We only have to pay for what we get with money substitutes (FRNs) because our suppliers usurped *our personal credit exemption* for their own use *when we fail to object* and do not demand *our personal credit exemption* for ourselves. *They can't use our credit when we object.*

All taxes are interest payments that accrue from the principle of our *personal credit* that we lend to the lending institutions of the corporate UNITED STATES, and these *interest payments* must be returned *to us, as the lenders of our personal credit*, if we claim them for the closing of escrow, lest we be found guilty *"for failing to make a return"* of that interest to us, that we could have claimed but did not.

My credit exemption is assured; it is my Super-sedeas Bond because:

"No state shall...make any...law impairing the obligation of contracts." — Art. 1, Sec. 10, clause 1, US Constitution.

18

The Truth Now Is Told

The corporate United States and its Subdivisions (Municipalities) have been operating in Chapter-11 bankruptcy reorganization since 1933. Since there was not enough gold and silver *"money of account of the United States"* to back the nation's currency, pay its debts, and enable the businesses of the United States to pay theirs, Congress passed laws that replaced the **substance money** needed to *'pay'* debts with **unredeemable paper promissory notes** issued by the non-federal Federal Reserve Bank to *'discharge'* debts instead.

Ordinarily this would have been a gross violation of the US Constitution that requires our currency to be backed by gold and silver coins, but it does **not violatie the Constitution in a bankruptcy reorganization,** which is a legal suspension of normal obligations, **for the protection of the debtor** (the corporate UNITED STATES) **from its creditors** (from we the people of the United States).

When Treasury notes come due they are not paid. They are **refinanced** by new Treasury Bills that back the currency and cover the debts.

You can't do that with debt that you owe unless you are protected from creditors in a bankruptcy reorganization that is regularly and constantly being restructured to keep the organization alive.

Congress legislated that *'new money'* shall be backed by *"the credit of the United States"* and represent *"a mortgage on all the...property of the people in the nation."*

So who holds the mortgage?

Under the Constitution and laws of equity the United States could not borrow or pledge the property and wealth of its *private citizens* and put them at risk as collateral backing the nation's currency and credit, *except in bankruptcy reorganization* where the *private citizens* become the Principals and *prime Creditors* of the United States and its subsidiaries holding a **REMEDY** for the recovery of interest due them *on their loan of credit to the public domain* — and this is what we have in HJR 192 of 1933.

As *prime Creditors* outside of the bankruptcy, we the citizens of the United States can not recover what is due us, in Federal Reserve Notes (FRNs), *without increasing the debt,* since there is no **"money of account of the United States"** (meaning gold and silver coin) *with which to exchange* ("pay") *tangible value* (substance) *for anything.*

Here were the America people at the heart of the depression in 1933 whose property and wealth were collateralizing the government's currency and debt, with no way to pay their debts with lawful **"money of account of the United States."**

So HJR 192 of 1933 mandates that *"a right to require payment in...a particular kind of coin or currency...is against Public Policy."*

This resolution allows the people who backed the *bankruptcy reorganization of the United States* with their credit (*meaning we the people*) to recover our equity by *discharging debts that we owe to subcorporate entities of the United States,* by corresponding *adjustments and set-*

offs of mutual credit exchanges against a "dollar for dollar" amount of United States debt and its sub-corporate entities, **owed back to us** through drafts, bills of exchange and promissory notes tendered for that purpose.

An arcane system, almost like barter, is still in effect today for those who discover it and access it.

Accordingly, the definition of legal tender includes *"circulating notes...of national banks"* which include **the holders of U.S. Corporate bankruptcy reorganizational debt,** who collectively and nationally constitute a *"national banking association"* or **"national bank,"** since 1933, *having the right to issue credit instruments to recover interest due them on the public debt.*

The government doesn't publicize this action for obvious reasons and they make it difficult to determine how to do this. **But the government will not dishonor a prime Creditor's presentment for remedial recovery via the REMEDY provided.**

The entire bankruptcy reorganization **continues** in equity **with our implied consent** backed by the credit of our assets and wealth — at risk as collateral for the currency and **national debt of the UNITED STATES and its sub-corporate entities** — because the **REMEDY** to recover what is due us as citizens is there . . . even though we are not told that it exists, **nor how to access it.**

*If the government were to ever **dishonor the REMEDY**, it would be a debtor seeking to operate outside of his bankruptcy reorganization plan, on the sly, **without clean hands** which is a criminal offense, for those responsible could eventually cause the entire government debt to we the people, the holders and creditors of the government, to be called due by us.*

This is another reason the government is afraid to be on record about our **Supersedeas Bond** lest someone says the wrong thing and brings disaster. **This is too sensitive and volatile a subject to take lightly.**

The individual creditor or sub-corporate entity operating within the bankruptcy who dishonors a holder's recovery of what is due him, in discharge of public debt, places himself outside of the bankruptcy's protection from its creditors in equity, and he is then open to **involuntary bankruptcy and liquidation of his assets** to the amount of the debt the principal creditor seeks to discharge, and to the full amount of that sub-corporate entity's share of the public debt owed to the prime creditors and holders of it, if he chooses to prosecute.

Notarial Protest and Dishonor are non-court administrative proceedings for the common citizen to initiate in a private capacity if necessary.

Every time the Federal Debt ceiling is raised by Congress they are restructuring the bankruptcy reorganization of the government's debt so that we can all continue in commerce.

The US Corporate public debt is trillions and trillions of dollars. The whole system is like a **house of cards** teetering in the wind and there are powerful unseen forces working at whatever cost to keep peace and good relations with **the Principals and Secured Parties** who provide the collateral for the country's currency, commerce and credit and who **hold the first mortgage on the nation** to keep all that we have going. **Therefore the processing of these instruments is a very sensitive delicate confidential private matter.**

The United States government doesn't want to have to

openly recognize all this, but when put in a position of legally having to acknowledge or deny it, ***those responsible will not deny it. To refuse a standing obligation of the United States would be a criminal act for them.*** Moreover, it would place the United States government ***operating outside its bankruptcy reorganization in violation of the law,*** and would collapse the entire financial system built on credit reorganization.

Be very discrete about sharing this information.
These ideas in the wrong hands can be a danger.

But the Secretary of the Treasury and those in charge cannot pay the debt either, for there is no money. To do so would be public testimony, official witness and admission by the government to the fact **that the REMEDY exists.**

Millions of people would start discharging their debts against the **REMEDY.** The result would be chaos!

Due to the sensitive nature of this ***constructive trust*** — created as a **REMEDY** for the ***Secured Party Creditors*** of the U.S. Corporate's reorganization debt — the government will not ever be able to pay it.

But they really don't have to.

As long as the government does not refuse, deny, return, or dishonor our discharge claims, they have accepted them and whether paid or not in law, they have permitted our claims of discharge ***to become legally enforceable obligations of the United States*** and the parties and banks involved can legally gain relief through the United States' regulatory avenues to obtain more credit, or release credit due customer's account.

This is not testimony or acknowledgment by the government of the **REMEDY,** because their silence does not indicate why they have remained silent.

Nevertheless, the government has provided practical means for recovery to we the people, *the prime Creditors and Holders of the National Debt.*

It is not likely that any agency or division of government under the direct or indirect control of the Secretary of the Treasury has dishonored by refusing to accept the instruments for which the United States is legally liable.

Fascinating isn't it?

The evidence of what is happening is all around us in the news every day. It is very impressive. *And it is best for us not to bring it up.*

Only show that you know it.

Just let it be *known* that you know.

> "Ye shall know the truth, and the truth shall set you free." — *Jesus the Christ, at John 8:32.*

19

Inflation, Interest & Taxation

Recorded by California Republic Chief Justice, Ken Cousens, Republic Call, July 13, 2011.

There are ***three things*** in our current monetary system that are purely scientific, and ***systematically designed to steal all of the wealth of all the people today,*** and what we're living in, in our social economic structure, is based on those three things: ***Inflation, Interest,*** and ***Taxation.***

With these ***three things,*** and with an elastic monetary system, the complete draining of virtually 98% of the wealth created by the people of America, by the banks, is taking place.

The fundamental of what we need to do in restructuring a balanced and a grounded foundational monetary system, with a currency, a treasury, and all of that, is to ***remove the things*** that basically lead to this stealing of the wealth.

So let me define elastic monetary currency. Elastic means that it is not fixed; it's not on a par (common level) with one-to-one direct value.

That word "par" is very important to understand, because there is something in the study of monetary structure called a "parity" system ("parity" meaning *equal* or *equivalent*). That means that one unit measurement of value, like a dollar, or a pound, or anything that measures value, is on par, equal one-to-one with a unit of wealth creation.

And there are only four main components of wealth creation: **Labor, Intellectual property, Natural resources** or *raw materials,* and **Manufacturing:** taking Labor, Intellectual property, and Raw materials; and producing a product, such as furniture, houses, automobiles, and all the rest of that.

So we have this term called Gross Natural Product (GNP), or Gross Domestic Product (GDP).

If we're in a parity system, then we create a unit of value, whether we call it a dollar, a sovereign, a beany, or whatever, and we issue that as money; because money is continually being created.

Once that **unit of value** is produced by human effort and natural resources, and a **unit of measure** is created, then we're on a parity system; one-to-one.

If those three incremental negative functions, **Inflation, Interest,** and **Taxation** are no longer part of the monetary system, since these are what create elasticity, we have a parity system where the wealth that is being created is retained by the people in the communities, and is building an economic basis that becomes stronger and stronger, is balanced, and does not involve the vast amounts of undermining forces that we're all experiencing today.

So where did we get an elastic monetary system? That's not how the founders started it. We started with what is called **standard weights** and **measures.**

We had a **bi-metal system** where gold and silver were pegged or fixed in a special ratio so that it could not be manipulated against paper.

So all through the 1800's the system was progressively eroded, silver was taken out as a monetary standard in the 1870's, and then into the early 1900's.

In 1913, the Federal Reserve Act was created, and within two years the United States corporation was put into bankruptcy, and the creditor was the Federal Reserve System — the 12 Federal Reserve Banks and their foreign owners who had put the United States into Bankruptcy, and required as part of the bankruptcy reorganization, the implementation of something called *legal tender,* with legal tender laws based on commerce.

And by 1965, the silver was removed as a circulating medium of coins, and in 1966, the international, Uniform Commercial Code (UCC) was introduced, creating a purely elastic currency.

From that point on, an ever-expanding and contracting of the monetary base, caused a steady reduction of the purchasing power of each individual unit of value, or dollar.

And through those three mechanisms, *Inflation, Interest,* and *Taxation,* a progressive *eroding of the wealth of the people* of the United States to the foreign owners of the non-federal Reserve *is taking place.*

So that elasticity is very important to understand, since during the history of the last 60-90 years, we see cycles of recessions and expansions at work.

When the bubble expands, the people go to work because of the fluidity of currency and the credit. We saw that in the 1990's in what became known as the "Dot-Com" bubble. The Stock Market created mere paper, along with the creation of capital and stock, and it expanded, then it contracted. Then in the 2000's we had the housing bubble and the mortgage bubble, to boot.

If you look back decade by decade, there were bubbles in mortgages, in farmland values, in commodities, etc. And when the bubbles would expand, the people would go to work, they would build houses, create farms, build manufacturing facilities, and when that elasticity pulled in and the bubbles broke, this would literally sweep away the wealth, like a windshield wiper that sweeps the water off with every motion, to be redistributed to the big corporations, until where we are fiscally today.

So, the Republic gives us now the ability to create a sound monetary policy through a balanced system that will create parity in the people's wealth, so that we can build and maintain that wealth, and can go back to the America that honored and supported innovation, the emergence of technology, education, and everything else that built this country to be what we knew it to be when we were growing up.

It is all too apparent, the corporate UNITED STATES is no longer the Leader of this world. So that's what we're doing in the Republic: creating a *lawful basis,* a *lawful enclave* to reintroduce a sound monetary policy and enable us to keep that wealth that we build.

20
The Debt-Money System

The three outstanding inventions that have contributed most to the evolution of mankind are and have been:

1. ***The invention of letters*** equipped man to crystallize his thoughts and record them in concrete form and develope his needs.

2. ***The invention of money*** as a medium of exchange by which his many needs could be conveniently met by exchanging money for the thinks he requires.

3. ***The invention of gunpowder*** equalized physical inequalities and made it no longer possible for the strong to impose his will upon the weaker.

Of these three, the invention of money is by far the most potent, for by the controlling of money the other forces come easily under domination.

Money is the most powerful 'thing' in the material world. This knowledge must remain private and not become public property. To properly do so, it is only necessary to control the press.

In a 'pleasure-mad' America the pursuit of ribald pleasures is the most important object of human attainment. 99% would sooner labor for 8-10 hours each day than spend 10 minutes of that same day in earnest mental concentration for advancement.

It is not difficult to keep the people ignorant of the money question. Its very simplicity makes it one of the most difficult subjects in political economy to understand.

Perhaps not one person in 1,000 knows or understands the definition of money. Most people see money as a measure or standard of value, or as representing property or wealth.

The truth is that money is worthless until it is exchanged for something desired. Money is a tool of exchange and nothing more. It transfers property from one person to another as a wagon hauls goods from one place to another.

Money has created the highly developed division of labor we have today. Money has made possible our highly specialized civilization.

Now, all commodities are first exchange for money, and this money is exchanged again for other commodities. Money is simply a medium of exchange. Money is the lifeblood of the economic world.

All other commodities become less in value (decrease in value) with the passing of time. Commodities are always in a hurry to sell, whereas money can wait, it is in no hurry to buy.

Money can therefore dictate the conditions of exchange, and business has no logical comeback, because our government overlooks this tribute power of money, changing it from commanding a useful servant into a dangerous master.

The true function of money is to serve the circulation and exchange of commodities. Money was never meant to tie up the marketplace, but this is exactly what it can do in a perfectly legal way, when its owners simply refuse to buy until their terms are met.

Thus money has become a monopoly that wields enormous power today.

If all lines of industry are flourishing and goods are being produced everywhere, the mere insufficiency of money to keep pace with production has a tendency to bring prosperity to a stand-still and bring about a depression.

By withdrawing vast sums of money from circulation, the law of supply and demand increases the buying power of the remaining money supply correspondingly.

Production is, and always has been, insufficient, but we hear today much *false* talk about of over-production.

The total demand for commodities in the economic sense is governed wholly by the amount of money in circulation whose owners are able and willing to buy, and nothing else.

Money control determines how much business there will be and if and when business ends; namely when there is no more money able and willing to buy.

Perhaps a still greater advantage money has over other commodities is its ability, through being hoarded and other schemes, to avoid the burden of taxation. Upon this factor more than any other depends the continuance of the advantage the moneyed class holds over the masses.

When the owner of a bushel of wheat exchanges that bushel of wheat in the market for money, the purchaser of the wheat becomes a ready target for the tax collector because his wheat is bulky and cannot be easily concealed.

What's more, the wheat is at all times subject to constant deterioration and therefore must be sold or used in a reasonable time, or it will eventually lose its value altogether. But not so with the seller of the wheat who is now in possession of the money, and this money can be easily hoarded and withdrawn from circulation and never depreciate in the manner in which other commodities depreciate.

In fact, the more money is hoarded, the more valuable it and the remaining money in circulation becomes. Also the holder of such money can and most always does avoid the payment of taxes on the money in his possession or under his control.

This is why it is so necessary to understand the laws and functions of money, and why we advocate the issuance of **interest free currency,** directly by the Treasury of the united States, in exchange for services rendered or property conveyed to the government by sale.

The adopting of this Plan would result in an immediate resumption of business and greatly lessen the unemployed, and ultimately lead to this Plan's universal adoption.

If such a thing as this is done, the international bankers would be hopelessly sunk. They are now drawing interest on billions of dollars of public debt, as evidenced by the various issues of outstanding national, state, and municipal bounds and corporate, farm and private loans.

The private banking system now holds bonds and mortgages far in excess of the present combined wealth of all the physical property in the United States.

The banking system is the vehicle through which the bankers control and manage these vast resources and collect tribute therefrom.

Through careful nursing of their ever-watchful representatives in Congress, this private banking system has become so systematized that it now controls the total volume of money in circulation and can drive the price of commodities up and down as its interests at the moment demand.

Such things as unemployment do not affect the private bankers in the least. In fact, they rebound to their benefit. The more unemployment, the more relief is sought from the banks. The more bonds, the more taxes. The more taxes, the more interest the bankers can clip from those bonds.

The only time bankers seem to be interested in unemployment and decreased industry is when their greater interest is in unloading the cheap commodities they have bought with their dear money. They then for a time restore the purchasing power to those who want to buy the commodities at greatly increased prices.

If the practical utility of a debt-free credit-money system — as opposed to the debt money system that they now impose — should become realized and demonstrated, even in the least, public opinion would soon demand the retirement of all national and state debts with 'honest money'; and the private bankers would no longer be able to enjoy the enormous benefits they enjoy, with their vaults full of interest amortizing (*depreciating*) free currency, and tax free government bonds.

21
Properties of Gold

Oh gold! Beautiful Gold! To you the friends of finance bow their heads in holy awe. To you mankind bends its knee in humble reverence.

For you nations have destroyed nations, traitors have betrayed their countries, and brothers have murdered brothers. Through you the friends of finance have made beggars of all mankind. May the splendor of your glory never wane.

Many times before in the history of mankind the moneyed or privileged class has been on the verge of accomplishing its great ambition of world domination, but each time it has become drunk with power and over-stepped the bounds of reason and lost its advantage.

Its members fail to lean the scriptural lesson of the 'talents'. They fail to demoralize their victims, they fail to sway them into their program by appealing to their magnanimity (loftiness of spirit, and sacrifice).

The use of gold as a standard of value is a trick of the financial wizard as old as the hills from which it came. It serves to keep the public attention focused away from the important movements that are forever taking place behind the scenes.

And yet, millions of businessmen in America today depend upon the uncertainty of some prospector finding enough gold upon which to base an emission of currency in sufficient quantities to care for increased and increasing business, in the hope of finding sufficient yield to enable an expansion of currency to back the money upon which the price of their manufactured products depend.

Gold is claimed and generally thought to be the most sought after thing in all the world. It is the magic talisman by which the financial wizards have first enticed, then awed, and finally subdued the un-initiate.

The intrinsic value of gold is just as valuable to mankind as he presumes it to be, when its true function and purpose are not understood.

It was at one time estimated that all the gold produced in the world, to that date, would not make a cube fifty-foot square. Yet with this insignificant quantity of gold in existence, the international bankers have been enabled to control the price of all commodities, and virtually govern the commerce of the world, to say nothing of world politics, by keeping the people deceptively ignorant of the laws (principles) governing the function of money, and by using that knowledge to manipulate and limit the volume of money in circulation at hand

It is only necessary to get the people to accept and believe the theory that to be stable, money must have an intrinsic value over and above the peoples' inherent credit. And strangely enough, this fallacy is the easiest thing to establish. Whereas the intrinsic value of the irredeemable paper dollar lies in the government's 'promise to pay'. In as much as it possess no intrinsic value at all, its value depends solely upon the faith and confidence of the people in which the government is held.

Money is merely a function of government; the thing that gives both money and the government the value that they possess is the sovereign stamp of the government's approval on each piece; that government's 'promise to receive' said money in payment of customs, taxes, and other government revenues.

The omission of this 'promise to receive' clause on the private so-called 'money' that we use today is one of the most fruitful sources of revenue that the international bankers enjoy. It enables them to get away with billions of dollars, annually, that they could not otherwise purloin (steal in violation of trust).

If they were compelled to put the clause below on the billions of private securities (money substitutes) which they unload upon the public each year, it would cost them those billions.

Suppose a bank or building and loan association holding ten million dollars of outstanding certificates of indebtedness, deposits, etc., goes into bankruptcy liquidation, none of these certificates which are the banks' obligations (expressed or implied), or debt 'promises to pay', carry the clause **"Receivable in payment of debts due the Corporation"**.

The bank has invested nothing in these securities as the collateral for the repayment of its loans. These securities have a collateral value far in excess of twice the amount of the loans, however, upon failure and liquidation of the bank, all their loans are immediately called due, and if the debtors are unable to pay or refinance their loans, foreclosure proceedings are immediately instituted and the property sold at great loss to the debtors — **with no loss to the banks.**

DebtOcracy

22
Colonial Script

Colonial history reveals that Benjamin Franklin went to England as a representative of the Colonies.

When the English officials asked him how it was, that the Colonies managed to collect enough taxes to build poor houses, and how they were able to handle the great burden of caring for the poor, Franklin's reply was most revealing:

"We have no poor houses in the Colonies, and if we had, we would have no one to put in them as in the Colonies there is not a single unemployed man; no poor, no vagabonds." This was in the year 1750 before the Revolutionary War. The United States had surpassed Britain in Commerce.

Think long and hard about this: in the American colonies before the America Revolution, there was *"not a single unemployed man; no poor, no vagabonds"* — no one on Welfare, no one on Social Security, no homeless, no income tax, no alphabet agencies, no IRS, BATF, FBI, DEA, CIA, HEW, OSHA, SBA, NEA, and on and on and on, to provide for the "general Welfare" of our villages, towns, cities and states.

How did Benjamin Franklin explain this to the British officials of his day?

This is how:

"It is because, in the Colonies, we issue our own paper money. We Call it Colonial Script. We issue only enough to move all goods freely from the Producers

to the Consumers. As we create our money, we control the purchasing power of money, and have no interest to pay."

This system guarantees LAWFUL MONEY. It was not controlled by **a private, for-profit corporation** with a monopoly on the credit of the nation as it is today.

There was no inflation or deflation, as long as the MONEY SUPPLY WAS KEPT EQUAL TO THE VALUE OF GOODS AND SERVICES TO BE PRODUCED AND MOVED ABOUT THE COUNTRY FOR HUMAN CONSUMPTION.

This system which Franklin described was taken away from the American colonies through the gradual encroachments of the British Parliament (the legislative branch of Britain's government) and the enforcement of this legislation in the King's Admiralty/Maritime/Equity courts in the colonies, without reference to the common law established by MAGNA CARTA that led to the America Revolution.

Those encroachments are described in the Declaration of Independence!

America today is being governed without reference to Magna Carta and our national and state Constitutions.

All of England's money, in Franklin's day, was borrowed from private banks at interest, and repressive taxes were laid upon the English people.

Private banks usurped the government's right to create and regulate money. Banks created money or credit "out of nothing", by mere bookkeeping entries, with no labor or wealth involved or exchanged.

England's money supply was not kept equal to the value of goods to be moved. Nor was it issued interest or tax free. It was issued at interest by private for-profit banks "out of nothing" just like it is being issued here in America today.

The enables the government to buy and control all major media; to buy and control even the government itself to serve its purposes.

Today, America and the rest of the world suffers from this same **debt money system.** We have all become **"servant/ slaves"** to the money lenders.

The people retain an inalienable right to create their own medium of exchange, through their elected representatives in the Congress of the United States as mandated by the U.S. Constitution.

When this right was challenged by the British, the Colonists went to war. Benjamin Franklin identified this as the real reason for the REVOLUTIONARY WAR of Independence. He said:

"The Colonies would gladly have borne the Stamp Act and the little tax on tea and other matters, had it not been that England took away from the Colonies their money, which created unemployment and dissatisfaction."

Here we see the cause of poverty, unemployment and financial insecurity. There can be no personal liberty without financial freedom.

Thomas Jefferson prophesied what would happened to America if we ever lost the inalienable right to issue our own money:

"If the American people ever allow private banks to control the issue of their money, first by inflation (creating the bubbles) *and then by deflation* (bursting the bubbles)*, the banks, and corporations that will grow up around them, will deprive the people of their property until their children will wake up homeless on the continent their fathers conquered."*

Jefferson's prophesy has come to pass here in the corporate UNITED STATES. America allows private banks to issue the nation's money. The non-federal Federal Reserve Bank issues our money, and is a for-profit International Bank. The banks and corporations have grown up around us and deprived us of our property.

How many Americans really own their own homes? The great majority of so-called "homeowners" pay rent via mortgage payments to the banks, and rent to the "government", via "property taxes" so-called. The "paid up" Deeds for the property that "owners" think they own, read that the owners are merely "Tenants"!

"We must not let our rulers load us with perpetual debt." If we run into such debts as that we must be taxed in our meat and in our drink, in our necessities and comforts, in our labors and in our amusements, for our callings and our creeds; our people must come to labor 16 hours in the 24, give the earnings of 15 of these to the government for their debts and daily expenses; and the 16th being insufficient to afford us bread."

"We have no time to think, no means of calling the mis-managers to account; but be glad to obtain subsistence by hiring ourselves out to rivet their chains on the necks of our fellow sufferers."

"Our landholders, too, retaining indeed the title and stewardship of estates, called heirs, but held really in trust for the treasury, are Tenants, THIS IS THE TENDENCY OF ALL HUMAN GOVERNMENTS."

"Has not a departure from principle become a precedent for a second? that second for a third? and so on, till the bulk of society is reduced to mere automa-

tons of misery, to have no sensibilities left but for sinning and suffering. And the fore horse of this frightful team is public debt. Reaction follows that, and in its train, wretchedness and oppression."

Our present day bureaucrats are glad to obtain subsistence by hiring themselves out to the banks to rivet the bank's chains on the necks of our fellow countrymen. It's happening today! Is not the public debt the fore horse of the taxation that has followed in its train?

Thomas Jefferson's prophesy has come to pass in America today!

"The system of banking we have is both equally and ever reprobated. I contemplate it as a blot lift in all our constitutions, which, if not covered, will end in their destruction. I sincerely believe, with you, that banking establishments are more dangerous than standing armies; and that the principle of spending money to be paid by posterity, under the name of funding, is but swindling futurity on a large scale."

Thomas Jefferson, in a letter to John Taylor, May 28, 1816, said"

"Has this 'blot left in our constitutions' been covered yet? Have our constitutions 'ended in destruction'"?

Thomas Jefferson, in another place, expanded on this.

"I believe that banking institutions are more dangerous to our liberties than standing armies. Already they have raised up a money aristocracy that has set the government at defiance to the people. THE ISSUING POWER SHOULD BE TAKEN FROM THE BANKS AND RESTORED TO WHOM IT PROPERLY BELONGS."

It belongs to the united States of America but was stolen by a crooked congressman, one Senator Nelson Aldridge — and Wall Street Bankers — in 1910.

The Republic for the united States of America has been Re-Inhabited, since March of 2010, to operate under the Plan of God, as the Founding Fathers ran our Government from 1776 to 1860, on Faith, Hope, Charity and Truth.

23

China Given Eminent Domain For United States Debt

Sources at the United States Embassy in Beijing China have confirmed that the United States of America has tendered to China a written agreement which grants to the People's Republic of China, an option to exercise Eminent Domain within the USA as collateral for China's continued purchase of US Treasury Notes and existing US Currency reserves.

The written agreement was brought to Beijing by Secretary of State Hillary Clinton and was formalized and agreed to during her recent trip to China.

This means that in the event the US Government defaults on its financial obligations to China, the Communist Government of China would be legally permitted to physically take, inside the USA, land, buildings and factories, perhaps even entire cities, to satisfy the financial obligations to China, of the US government.

Put simply, the feds have now actually mortgaged the physical land and property of all citizens and businesses in the United States. They have given to a foreign power, the constitutional power to "take" all of our property, as collateral for continued Chinese funding of US deficit spending and the continued carrying of US national Debt.

This is an unimaginable betrayal of every man, woman and child in the USA. An outrage worthy of violent overthrow.

In other words: Should the United States corporation default on financial obligations, land, buildings, factories and even entire cities will be taken by the Communist Government. It's all been planned out through years of planning.

There is no real plan to pay back this debt, therefore property will be bought up by creditors for pennies on the dollar.

China began its covert challenge to the United States corporation in the 1950's by taking over much of the manufacturing of pharmaceutical drugs for American and British Big Pharma that was an outgrowth of the Rothschild's opium-ring processing by the British West Indies Company during the 1800's, and is brokered by the "City of London" and Washington, DC.

The eventual President of the LDS Church (Mormon), Gordon B. Hinckley, via the church-owned Polynesian Cultural Center in Hawaii established a hard currency pipeline with Bejing, China, for exchanging bank trade credits for CIA/ British M16 drug services rendered into hard gold and silver while hiding behind the cloak of World Religion.

This is being facilitated via the LDS-Church-built and controlled Shenzhen Special Economic Zone adjacent to Hong Kong.

When Hinckley was made LDS President, his first official visit, as World Prophet, was to China, where the Chinese Communist leaders gave him a hero's welcome and confetti parade.

Arkansas natives Bill Clinton and Sam Walton massively increased contracts with China's factories over 2,000%. This resulted in a tremendous imbalance of U.S. trade with China.

Thanks to the Mormon Special Economic Zone, China's leaders began to amass incredible real wealth in silver and gold. With this incredible real wealth provided by the Shenzhen Economic Zone exchanges, China has purchased trillions of dollars worth of U.S. Treasury Bills and Bonds.

Much of the U.S. national debt has been purchased from the non-federal Federal Reserve Banks in this manner.

In December, 2005, the Chinese Defense Minister, Chi Haotiaon delivered a speech to Chinese military leaders outlining the inevitable expansion of China into Canada, Australia, and the United States. He justifies this because of Chinese racial superiority, and thus eminent domain.

Eminent domain is "the inherent power of a governmental entity to take privately owned property, esp. land, and convert it to public use, subject to reasonable compensation for the taking". (Black's Law 7th, p. 541).

To accomplish this, America would supposedly first have to be "cleansed" by means of a powerful biological weapon causing 150-200 million American deaths.

Dr. Jeff Taubenberger, of the U.S. Institute of Pathology in Ft. Dedrick MD, the world headquarters for biological weapons development, successfully mapped the genome of the 1918 killer flue virus responsible for the 1918 pandemic that killed millions. The worst killer virus ever to plague mankind is now ready to be used as a covert "weapon" disquised as a natural influenza mutation.

On March 13, 2008, a secret meeting was conducted for the U.S. House and Senate where agents of the Club of Rome gave a preview of upcoming events to elected officials who first had to swear an oath of secrecy regarding those details.

The traitors were briefed that the economy would begin to collapse in October, 2008, and would totally collapse in mid 2009. As events unfolded in 2009-2010, Congress was told about the real possibility of massive civil unrest and even Civil War being waged. Detention camps have now been constructed to imprison civil 'agitators'.

See http://www.afterdowningstreet.org/node/34877 for the complete meeting agenda.

In September, 2008, as soon as the Olympics were concluded, China stopped buying oil and gas futures and began dumping U.S. Treasury bills and bonds. Gasoline prices plummeted, while the U.S. mortgage loan money became tightly constricted. The Club of Rome's agenda was being implemented perfectly.

In October, just as explained in March, the economy indeed began to collapse with mortgage banks going bankrupt as the Chinese dumped their U.S. Securities. This caused a world-wide "rush to liquidity" as money supplies drastically tightened.

Billions of worthless U.S. Government "bailout" debt entries were given to bolster failing U.S. Banks. These were worthless because China now controls most of the U.S. real wealth in the form of silver and gold.

After China refused to continue investing in credit loans to the U.S. Treasury, China agreed to continue investing in U.S. Treasury Bills after being given in exchange the right of "eminent domain" to physically repossess foreclosed American private property in the event of default.

This gives the Chinese military the legal right to use biological weaponry to "clean up America all at once". It gives them the legal right to use deadly force in removing trespassing Americans from occupying Chinese/American real estate.

In early February, nine U.S. States began the process of re-asserting their sovereignty pursuant to the Ninth and Tenth

Amendments to the US Constitution, declaring null and void any actions by Congress that have violated or violate the Constitution.

The state took action to make certain the feds couldn't give away cities, or the states themselves.

This situation could get ugly very fast as one sovereign power (the feds) try to literally give away the land of other sovereign powers (the states). This is the type of thing that starts Civil Wars.

It may even bring the actors in Congress to their senses to see that the **"debt-money-system"** being used by the bankers today, needs to be reformed into the **"credit-money-system"** recommedned in this book; that will allow us to **"pay"** debts with real *"money of account of the united States"* — *for the American Republic.*

DebtOcracy

24

Insolvent United States

In late May, in response to the growing debate over rais-
ing the debt ceiling, the Treasury Department issued a press
release telling the world what it largely already knew: The
United States is insolvent and lacks the assets to pay its
debts.

According to Treasury officials, the United States is borrowing $125 billion dollars a month, much of it to pay inter-
est on existing debt. Even if Congress were to decide to
liquidate American taxpayers' assets in a fire sale, including gold reserves, mortgage-backed securities and assets
such as stock in automakers and other big companies, it
would not be able to raise enough money quickly enough to
counterbalance the amount it needs to borrow to stay sol-
vent.

The United States bases its currency on debt. The government issues Treasury bonds that are bought by private
investors, including the non-federal Federal Reserve. The
Federal Reserve, a network of private banks, issues U.S.
currency at interest as obligations against its assets, particularly Treasury bonds.

In the current economic situation, the United States has
been reducing the productivity of its population by sending
jobs overseas while bringing into the country illegal immi-
grants to reduce the value of jobs within its borders.

In order to maintain the illusion of a higher standard of
living, Congress liberalized credit laws over the past few
decades, allowing citizens to borrow money that made up

for the income they were no longer receiving at their jobs.

However, by replacing jobs with bank "credit" (actually bank debt) and reducing the value of labor within its own economy, the U.S. reduced the tax base that is required to service its debt while increasing expenses that it has to service. These two forces collided in the ongoing economic crisis.

America does not have assets sufficient to make a substantial dent in its debt and faces a tax base and labor pool that is rapidly declining in value. As skilled jobs have been gutted by middlemen making deals with China, and domestic labor values have plummeted because of immigration policies, Congress is approaching a lead-in to the inevitable, which is either a U.S. default on its debt or a major devaluation of its currency.

Repudiation of its odious debt needs to be considered now.

Due to the UNITED STATES Inc. being in a State of Re-ceivership since its Bankruptcy of 1933, and its 14 trillion dollar debt — aside from other Countries in the same or worse economic conditions and the plan and goal of the New World Order to destroy America and reduce it to a third world country and to build a mega-freeway from Mexico to Canada through the middle of the U.S.A. — is it any wonder as to what's coming? And most of the American people have no clue!

DebtOcracy

25
New Federal Reserve Notes
Ready For Circulation

The United States Federal Reserve bankers are already prepared for a hostile merger of Canada with the United States. The same bankers who orchestrated the United States Wall Street swindle — the $12.5 trillion dollar bailout the Federal Reserve bankers swindled from the American taxpayers, December 1, 2010 — are laying in wait until Canada, the Canadian flag, and the Canadian Dollar are dissolved.

The Federal Reserve's North American Union Note has already been printed to replace the US Federal Reserve Note, the Canadian Dollar, and the Mexican Pesco.

Why is the Federal Reserve printing North American Union Notes?

The United States is financially bankrupt — thanks entirely to the Federal Reserve Bankers, who orchestrated the largest swindle in the history of the United States and the World, by fraudulently declaring bank loses of billions of dollars.

These bankers fraudulently declared that their banks would fail unless the US government paid them trillions of dollars in bailout money. Both George W. Bush and Barack Obama were willing conspirators in the massive swindle of over $12.5 trillion dollars from the American taxpayers.

Because Bush and Obama handed over trillions of dollars to the Federal Reserve bankers, the United States has no money to finance its social programs, its health care system, the American peoples' pensions, its military, its government, and all of its financial obligations.

The Japan earthquake and tsunami added to the US economic woes as the second largest holder of US debt can no longer support the US economy with loans. Japan is itself faced with the massive financial burden of rebuilding, and can no longer afford to buy US debt. China can clearly see that the US financial system is effectively insolvent; and is now starting to dump the worthless US federal Reserve Note.

The Federal Reserve bankers have been working for years to destroy the United States as we know it. Their goal is to bankrupt the United States through debt. By bankrupting the US, the US government will be forced to dissolve the United States Constitution and the Bill of Rights in favor of a North American Union with Canada and Mexico.

As the United States is the largest *forced trading partner with Canada* (NAFTA forcibly took control of the Canadian commerce), the Federal Reserve bankers have been preparing and are ready to force Canada into merging with the US to form a North American Union – one country, controlled by the non-federal Federal Reserve bankers.

A Stephen Harper majority in Canada was the key to forming the Federal Reserve bankers' "North American Union".

When Stephen Harper won only a minority government in 2008, the Federal Reserve bankers' plans for a takeover of Canada, in 2009, were defeated. In 2008 the Feds were so sure that Harper would win a majority, that they printed billions of dollars in North American Union Notes dated 2009.

The accompanying photo is a sample of the 2009 Federal Reserve North American Union Note. The counterfeit note is concrete evidence of the Federal Reserve bankers' conspiracy to destroy the United States, in order to form a non-federal Federal Reserve banker-controlled North American Union.

The Note Reads – "Federal Reserve Note."

It has the Federal Reserve banker adopted NAU flag (blue with 3 white stars that represent Mexico, the United States, and Canada) above the words "The United Federation of North America".

Below it, the Federal Reserve bankers boldly claim "THIS NOTE IS LEGAL TRANSNATIONAL TENDER BY UNION OF THE NORTH AMERICAN REPUBLIC **ESTABLISHED AND AUTHORIZED BY THE FREE TRADE AND RECOVERY ACT OF THE CENTRAL BANK** APPROVED BY THE U.S. FEDERAL RESERVE, BANQUE DU CANADA AND BANCO DE MEXICO".

The note is a complete fraud. In the United States – *"The Congress shall have Power to lay and collect taxes [and] to coin money, [and] regulate the value thereof. (Art.1 § 8).*

The Federal Reserve bankers' NAU Note unlawfully eliminates the US Congress power to coin the US money. The Noted is a fraud because it eliminates the vote of the US citizens, the Canadian citizens, and Mexican citizens. Its claim of legal tender is based entirely on the Federal Reserve created free trade agreement.

The Federal Reserve bankers claim totalitarian authority over the Canadian, Mexican, and United States people. Their worthless North American Union Note have never been approved by the people of Canadia, Mexico, and United States. The North American Union Note is only approved by itself.

It fraudulently claims that it is approved by the US, Canadan and Mexican central banks. Those central banks could never approve such a scheme as they are mandated by the elected representatives of the people of those three Countries.

In Canada the mandate of the *Bank of Canada* (*Banque Du Canada*) is to conduct monetary policy in a way that promotes the economic and financial well-being of Canadians – not to a foreign owned private non-federal Federal Reserve Bank.

What does this mean for Canadians? It gives Canadians another good reason not to give Stephen Harper a majority government.

26
God, Money & Lies

By Jerry Day of *Meetrix News*.

I have no idea why people have faith in God, or anything else they can't see or touch. I'm not religious. But I've noticed that many people who subscribe to the supremacy and authority of God, are starting to have a problem with the supremacy and authority of Government.

They feel that they can only serve one master. They feel that to serve two masters requires the betrayal of one of the masters for the benefit of the other, an impossible conflict.

As Government presumes more and more authority, it casts itself in the role of God. And that conflict grows greater.

Our Government tortures, kidnaps, assassinates, engages in slave trade through taxes of wages and earnings, and puts innocent citizens in bondage to [odious] debt without their consent.

Our Government, the one we pay for, the one we created, is doing things that the Bible says good men may not do.

On our dollar, it says "In God We Trust". That expression was not used by our forefathers to affirm their religion. Our nation's founders did not have the slightest doubt in the existence of God. They put that expression on the money as a defiant declaration against King George the 3rd that we choose to trust God, and not any king or government.

It meant that we recognize that God created man with unalienable rights, and man created government under him with no rights and limited authority.

For government to assume any authority over man is inverted reasoning and involves presumption. As an example of government's false presumption, right on this dollar bill, we are told this is money, it says dollar.

I looked at an old law dictionary, and it said that money is measured in gold and silver. If it is not gold or silver, it is not money, under the law. Well, the dollar is *not* gold or silver, nor is it backed by gold or silver; but must have value of some kind.

The Federal Reserve prints them, loans them out, and demands them back with interest. There must be some value there. Surely the Federal Reserve is not so greedy and criminal as to charge our government interest on something that has no value?

Fortunately, the Federal Reserve did explain the fundamentals of its money a few years ago in a bulletin called Modern Money Mechanics. So let's see what the creator and lender of your 'dollar' said about its value.

"In the United States neither paper currency, nor deposits have any value as commodities." That means that both your cash and your bank account have no intrinsic value. They are in fact worthless in legal and economic and practical terms. The only reason that Federal Reserve Notes can function at all as currency is, quote, "the confidence that people have that they will be able to exchange them for real goods and services."

So the Federal Reserve, the originator of our currency, has admitted that Federal Reserve Notes have absolutely no value outside of our imaginations.

So much for Federal Reserve propaganda; that was the good news. The truth is much worse than that. When you receive Federal Reserve Notes, to you they have *negative* value. They are damaged to you. When you get a dollar, you are not getting money, you are getting . . . you are trading your labor, goods or services for an obligation of debt.

At the very top of the dollar it does not say Federal Reserve Money, or Federal Reserve Currency. It says Federal Reserve Note, as in promissory note. If you're familiar with promissory notes, you will recognize the creditor's name goes at the top. The debtors name, just below the signature of the debtor's representative and witness and the enumeration of the debt.

That is not a dollar. It is an I.O.U. for a dollar. An instrument of debt and an obligation of the United States Government, and by taking possession of it, you become a debtor.

Your government borrowed that dollar at interest, and promised that you would pay the interest through all kinds of taxes, fees, fines, licenses, permits, judgements, and demands. As the Federal Reserve said, the dollar is not a commodity; it is a contract of debt attaching itself to anyone who touches it.

That contract says that those notes may be taken from you at the whim of government. Anything you buy with it may be confiscated by government. It's fools 'money'.

The Federal Reserve Note is the shackle and gun of the slave system known as fiat currency. The Federal Reserve Banks have trapped our government into constantly begging for more and more loans and to push worthless notes on ever American in a snowballing crisis of public debt and toxic currency.

This note is the single most destructive force against our

economy, wealth and freedoms, and our opportunities, not to mention the integrity of our government's finances. It is truly a system of bondage and economic suffocation.

Most Americans are fully brainwashed and think this is money. The hour is late, and the problem is massive (acute). Any solution now will have to be as large as the problem.

So it's time for all of us who care about our future to start imagining a world where we no longer use debt, and we no longer use unbacked currencies.

And most important of all, that we never again allow our government to borrow.

27

It's Only A Game
(It Can Be Deadly!)

**All systems of belief are a series of events charac-
terized by the birth of a good, or bad idea.** This idea
gradually develops into dogma devised by other human
beings, and finally ends up carved into the stone of **"you-
must-adhere-to-our-rules-or-else,"** by still more humans.

The original concept came from a human being just like
you and me. He simply had a revolutionary idea about how
the world should work and shared his idea with others.

Those people then take his idea and run with it and eventually develope it into their **"Rules Carved in Stone"**.

Absolutes make people feel safe.

So-called absolutes, **to the believer,** can't be argued
with, challenged, or changed.

Wars are fought over whose absolute Truth is the right
one. The debate over **which text is correct** has been the
number-one cause of violent death in the **long-time favor-
ite** Game of . . . **I'M RIGHT! and YOU'RE WRONG!**

Therefore, if it's only a Game, then we all have a part in it
to play. This author's part is to remind you that **"it's only a
Game."**

A certain game-player once told this story, about **"Monopoly"** — the money game that everyone plays. And while
visiting with friends, he was invited to play the game of **"Monopoly"** — but he declined.

His highly competitive host began to taunt him about his abilities, *and what-not.* After a few minutes of taunting, he replied, *"All right, I'll join you in your money game, but you won't like how I play."*

With that, they set up the game of "Monopoly" for four players. And after a time — all players having accumulated property to one degree or other — our hero unfortunately landed on one of his host's very expensive squares and became liable for a heavy property tax. The host smiled with cunning satisfaction, and glee, and put out his hand to receive the monopoly money.

"We can play this hand in two ways," says the man, *"You can let me go on, and we'll forget about the tax, or you can TAKE the money from me . . . in which case I will give ALL of my properties to Bob, over there, and he will undoubtedly win the game."*

"You can't do that," said the host, *"It's against the rules."*

"I'll tell you what," our hero replied, *"if you can find the rule that says I can't do it . . . I'll hand over the tax and we'll continue the game."*

Of course, the host dug out the rule book and pored through it like a mad-man-possessed, but — sure enough — there was no rule for or against our hero's tactic.

Realizing he was beaten, and not being prepared to let anyone else win by default, the host reliquished his right to take the tax and they played on.

Every time our man landed on another's property, he made the same offer and each player let him pass untaxed. He eventually won by a long margin, and laughed as he reminded them, *"I said you wouldn't like how I play."*

The Lesson Learned

By deferring to rules that others have set, and by following those rules to the letter, **because it seems safer to do so,** we risk being hampered and bound by those rules.

The Key is in trusting your own ability to fly "by the seat of your pants" (intuition). Then, you *realize* that you can **'level the field'** by using your mind . . . instead of deferring to others in the game.

An important part of enjoying the game, is in knowing what the rules are, and what they are not, and in never compromising the integrity of the game.

So *who-ever wins, in the end . . . it is YOU.*

And they hesitate to change the wheel!

Definition

odious interest. n. unconscionable interest deserving hatred or repugnance.

DebtOcracy

The American diplomats finally proved that Iraq's debt was odious and that the Iraqi people were not obliged to pay it.

However, Washington suddenly realized that they'd pried open a can of worms. For the first time in the 21st century, the ultimate Super Power had legitimized the concept of "odious debt".

So they chose to sweep this case under the rug.

DebtOcracy

The dictatorship of the bankers and their debt-money system are not limited to one country, but exist in every country in the world. They are working to keep their control tight, since one country freeing itself from this dictatorship and issuing its own *interest- and debt-free currency,* setting the example of what an honest system could be, would be enough to bring about the worldwide collapse of the bankers' swindling debt-money system.

NESARA: National *Economic Security and Reformation Act*
http://tinyurl.com/c8u42q6

History of Banking: *An Asian Perspective*
http://tinyurl.com/boeehjl

The People's Voice: *Former Arizona Sheriff Richard Mack*
http://tinyurl.com/d62fyg3

Asset Protection: *Pure Trust Organizations*
http://tinyurl.com/btrjfqp

The Matrix As It Is: *A Different Point Of View*
http://tinyurl.com/ckrbkge

From Debt To Prosperity: *'Social Credit' Defined*
http://tinyurl.com/d2tjmw3

Give Yourself Credit: *Money Doesn't Grow On Trees*
http://tinyurl.com/d7tphuv

My Home Is My Castle: *Beware Of The Dog*
http://tinyurl.com/bmzxc2n

Commercial Redemption: *The Hidden Truth*
http://tinyurl.com/d9etg7w

Hardcore Redemption-In-Law: *Commercial Freedom And Release*
http://tinyurl.com/cl65vrz

Oil Beneath Our Feet: *America's Energy Non-Crisis*
http://tinyurl.com/btlzqxf

Untold History Of America: *Let The Truth Be Told*
http://tinyurl.com/bu9kjjc

Debtocracy: *& Odious Debt Explained*
http://tinyurl.com/cooqzuz

New Beginning Study Course: *Connect The Dots And See*
http://tinyurl.com/cxpk42p

Monitions of a Mountain Man: *Manna, Money, & Me*
http://tinyurl.com/cusgcqs

Maine Street Miracle: *Saving Yourself And America*
http://tinyurl.com/d4yktlw

Reclaim Your Sovereignty: *Take Back Your Christian Name*
http://tinyurl.com/cf5taxh

Gun Carry In The USA: Your Right To Self-defence
http://tinyurl.com/cdn3y3y

Climategate Debunked: *Big Brother, Main Stream Media*
http://tinyurl.com/d6gy2xz

Epistle to the Americans I: *What you don't
know about The Income Tax*
http://tinyurl.com/d99ujzm

Epistle to the Americans II: *What you don't
know about American History*
http://tinyurl.com/cnyghyz

Epistle to the Americans III: *What you don't
know about Money*
http://tinyurl.com/cp8nrh8

www.ingramcontent.com/pod-product-compliance
Lightning Source LLC
Chambersburg PA
CBHW051532170526
45165CB00002B/701